Find Your Calling without Losing Your Mind

&

Overcome the Obstacles and Succeed at Your Calling

(Books 1 & 2 in the Find Your Calling Series)

By Christopher Wells

Author's blog: www.fictionwithamission.com

For a current list of titles by this author, visit http://fictionwithamission.com/books-by-c-l-wells/

Author's email address:
CLWells@fictionwithamission.com

Works of fiction by the author:

The Re-education of Senator X (Short Story)

Murder at Rendsburg Resort (Cozy Mystery)

Dylan & Faedra: The Super-Not Chronicles (YA)

Domestic Bliss (Sci-fi Short Story)

The Testament Stone (Paranormal Murder Mystery)

The Tucson Prophecy (Prequel to the Paranormal Gift Series)

The Seer (Book #1 in the Paranormal Gift series)

Utopian Day (International Crime Thriller)

Get your FREE Book

Visit this link for your FREE book:

http://fictionwithamission.com/go/free-book
(Note: The current free title may be different than the book pictured above)

Table of Contents

Book 1: Find Your Calling without Losing Your Mind

Book 2: Overcome the Obstacles and Succeed at Your Calling

Chapter 1 -
Crucial Questions about Finding Your Calling

Not long ago, I was listening to the story of a young Syrian refugee on the radio. He was being interviewed about the fact that he was a stand-up comedian and how that was a markedly different career path from what his family, and even he had once envisioned. At one point in the interview, he made statements along the lines of the following: "I would give up anything for stand-up comedy – anything. I have finally found what I think most people are looking for. I've found the thing in life that I was meant to do."

Like this young Syrian refugee, there are many of us on a similar quest to find answers to the questions, "Why am I here, and what am I meant to do in life?" This book was written to help enable you to find those answers for yourself.

I struggled for many years with this whole idea of calling and purpose in my own life. I know the inner drive that many of us have to answer these questions. I also know the intense dissatisfaction and depression that can result when those questions are not answered correctly - or not answered at all.

I am happy to say that I now have the answers to these questions in my own life, and - more importantly for you - I now have the tools and knowledge to help you answer these questions for yourself. What does that mean for you? No more pursuing some decoy-calling only to find you've wasted years doing something you aren't really passionate about and were probably never meant to do. No more struggling to find your calling and living every day with the disappointment of knowing that you haven't yet identified what it is. With God's help and some homework on your part, I can help you navigate the process of finding your calling once and for all—without you losing your mind in the process! And once you have found that calling, I can teach you how to be a success at it.

From a Christian worldview, the answer to these two questions would seem simple: 'I was created to have a relationship with God, and I am here to learn to love God and others.' And, yes, I believe this, at the most basic level, is why all human beings are here on planet Earth. However, there is something in the spiritual DNA of humankind that is not satisfied with that generic answer alone. There is some knowing in the heart of every human being that tells us with certainty that, in some way, each of us is different from every other human being who has ever lived. And, as such, we were created to live out that general purpose in our own specific way - a way that is as uniquely different from anyone else's life just as every snowflake that has ever been created is uniquely different from the next.

Most of us have an understanding in the core of our being, telling us that we each have our own specific mission to accomplish while we are here.

When you find that purpose—that calling—which is specific to you as an individual, you'll find yourself in that enviable place of waking up each morning with a sense of hope, fulfillment, and purpose that makes life's challenges and struggles meaningful and worth the effort. Living out your individual purpose is not always easy - far from it. But, when you are living out your calling in relationship and partnership with a loving, all-powerful God, you'll have an internal, quiet strength that fuels your progress, a sense of fulfillment, and a sense that you are living the life you were created to live.

So, what is different in the approach detailed in this book that sets it apart from every other 'find your purpose' book out there? Well, for starters, I'm not going to ask you to take a test, discover your Biblical 'spiritual gift', or give you any other such supposed short-cut. What I *will* do is offer you the insights and understanding that I have gained through successfully discovering and finding fulfillment in living out my own personal calling in life, and help equip you with the tools, knowledge, and beliefs that will help you do the same.

No single person's life experience is exactly the same as anyone else's. Therefore, the set of beliefs and assumptions about life which we arrived at this point in time are not identical to anyone else's. It may seem simplistic to point this out, but discussions about purpose and calling often ignore this fact that plays such a vital role in the process of discovering and living out one's calling.

In taking this journey, it will be necessary to embrace certain beliefs that will be easier for some people than for others. For instance, it may be easy for one person to believe in a loving Heavenly Father if that person had a good earthly father. However, for another person who had an abusive earthly father, choosing to believe in a loving Heavenly Father might be a Herculean task requiring great faith.

Our beliefs are a result of our own individual experiences and how we've processed those experiences. These beliefs significantly affect how we make this journey of discovery to find our calling and purpose in life. There are things we believe that may help us along that path, and there are things we believe that can hinder us. A large part of my own journey of discovery involved discarding the lies I had believed in for so many years—all the lies surrounding calling and purpose—and discovering and embracing the truths I needed to believe in in order to succeed. If you have struggled to find your own calling in life, the same sort of process will be necessary for you, as well.

This is the book I wish someone had given me as a younger man. It would have saved me years of frustration, depression, and disappointment, and helped me live a more fulfilling, productive, and satisfying life much sooner. However—as God can turn even our mistakes and detours into something good—I am now able to use those years of wandering in the wilderness of self-doubt and uncertainty to help you avoid the same pitfalls that I encountered.

In the coming chapters, I'm going to be sharing my personal story and using it as a springboard to illustrate the truths I've learned. As we progress, I'll discuss critical discoveries that I made and how these revelations can help you in your journey to find your calling. Finally,

I'll outline a plan to follow, breaking down the entire process for you in detail, so that you can better understand each part and have a blueprint to achieve success for yourself.

This is a journey of self-discovery and healing. It is a journey into the heart and mind of God during which you will discover truths you didn't know about your Creator. Along the way, you'll likely discover some lies you have believed *about* God as well. It is a journey of hope and of faith. I'm excited about being your guide, and feel privileged to assist you in this process.

So, let's begin.

Chapter 2 - The Journey Begins

As a young child, my parents would tell me that I was created for something special, but outside of their general instructions for me to live a Christian life, they never gave me a clear idea of what that something special might be. Since I'd been old enough to understand words, I had been schooled in the stories of the heroes of the Bible and how God had also created them for special tasks and assignments. In the context of this environment, I began to formulate my own ideas about what special purpose I might have been created to fulfill.

My earliest memories of attempting to fill in the blank regarding anything remotely resembling a calling revolve around the possibility of being a preacher. My father was a preacher; I looked up to him, and I identified with the idea of spreading the good news about

God and salvation through Christ Jesus. I remember, as a young boy, creating sermons in preparation for the day that I, too, would be a preacher like my father.

That initial idea of one day becoming a preacher, in one form or another, was to be a consistent theme in what I believed I was called to do and be for decades to come. As I became a teenager, I became interested in music and began writing songs which I then sang in the local church. I began to think that perhaps music ministry might be my calling.

Also in my teenage years, identifying my individual calling began to become a more prominent and important theme in my life. After all, the heroes of the Bible had each had a specific calling that was given to them, and they'd gone on to accomplish great things for God. They'd had a purpose. Certainly, they'd faced challenges, but with God's help, they'd overcome those challenges and most of them had ended up as heroes or heroines by the end of their stories. Why should I be any different? If I was truly special, as I had been raised to believe, then I should receive a confirmation of my calling, too. I began to wonder when I would receive this confirmation and be launched on the journey of a lifetime, accomplishing great things for God's kingdom.

The various churches I attended in my youth fanned the flames of this viewpoint of calling and purpose. I can remember many teachings and even written tests that were given in order to help us identify our spiritual gifts so that we could fulfill our God-given purpose in helping advance the kingdom of God. The idea seemed to be that once you had identified your spiritual gifts, then you could find your groove and reach your maximum level of productivity and fulfillment as a Christian.

I don't recall much about the actual findings of any of those tests that I took regarding spiritual gifts. However, I do recall that I was eager to get the results. I also remember being frequently disappointed when the results didn't seem to satisfy my desire to clarify, with any level of certainty, what my individual calling and purpose in life were.

By this point in my journey, I wasn't entirely convinced about what I was supposed to do with my life. I still felt, at the time, that it was something to do with Christian ministry – perhaps it was being a preacher or singer/songwriter/performer, but I was looking for confirmation to drive away the self-doubt. While I wasn't completely aware of the process that was taking place, I had subconsciously begun to form some very definite ideas about how my calling and purpose would be revealed. I began to believe that, if I was faithful in using the gifts that I had, one day God would metaphorically shine the light down from Heaven, and suddenly things would take off. I would suddenly be 'discovered' as one of the next great singers/songwriters/performers or spiritual teachers. This event, when it happened, would be the confirmation that I had been looking for that would affirm—once and for all—what my true calling was. After all, wasn't this what the Bible taught?

I had internalized what I thought were truths about calling from the stories of the Bible. Moses was a sheepherder on the back side of the desert one day, and then he had the burning bush experience that launched him on a mission to lead a nation from slavery to freedom. David was, similarly, a sheepherder who suddenly had a prophet anoint him to be the next King of Israel, launching him in his own calling and in a very definite direction. Paul was going about his business of persecuting the followers of Christ, and then he was thrown to the ground by a blinding light and had a personal encounter with Jesus Christ. That encounter forever changed his life and launched him on his own calling, which resulted in the spreading of the gospel to the known world. He even ended up writing two-thirds of the New Testament. And what about Mary? An angelic visitation confirmed that she would be the mother of the Savior of the world—Jesus Christ. You can't get a clearer confirmation of calling and purpose than that!

These are some of the better-known stories, but I could go on and on with many more. In each case, the hero or heroine had an experience which clearly conveyed to them what their calling was, and that experience forever altered the course of their lives. Beginning in my early teens and continuing through my early forties, I was living in expectation of my own divine 'calling encounter'. While I believed God had given me gifts, which I was currently using in ministry, I was still looking for my calling to be confirmed by either breakout success or some other encounter with God that would forever eliminate any doubt as to what I was really called to do in life.

At one point in this process, I went to the pastor of the church we were attending at the time and asked him to train me in the ministry. Honestly, I wanted to help build God's kingdom, and I just didn't feel fulfilled as a church attendee who was only involved in a ministry or two. I still had this gnawing certainty that I was meant for something more, but I hadn't yet found 'it' – whatever 'it' was.

That request ended up with me becoming a licensed minister and the associate pastor at the church. I definitely felt that 'this must be it'. Eventually, years later, my wife and I left that church to plant another church. It was a disaster on many levels. If you can come up with a list of what *not* to do when planting a church, I think you would find I accomplished the task with flair!

It is fair to say that, after that experience, I was at a low point in my life. Certainly, with regard to any calling or purpose, I was at a loss. After the experience of failing to successfully plant a church and the resultant destruction I had helped achieve in my marriage, I was simply trying to survive.

At that point, my wife and I began attending another church in the area, and we slowly began re-building our personal lives from the aforementioned carnage. Eventually, after months of spiritual triage, we started becoming involved in ministry once again. As time progressed, we became more and more invested. We taught classes, we helped with outreach, I preached on occasion, I helped out with the worship team on occasion, we discipled others in the faith, we were on the prayer team, et cetera. And in the midst of all of this, God was blessing our efforts. *Good things happened*. God used us to help others, and we were using our gifts to help build the kingdom of God. By all external standards, and even in my own mind and heart, I felt like I was gaining traction again, that I was hitting a groove which I would embrace as a calling.

This trend of successful ministry continued for several years. Yet, something was missing. And then, I believe God gave me a wonderful gift—He let me fail once again.

Had the things I was involved in at our church and via related Christian ministries continued to find much success, I might never have found my true calling. God, in His infinite wisdom, arranged for that not to happen. Over the course of about a year, every single endeavor I was involved in that revolved around anything I perceived as my calling experienced some level of failure—and some of them were spectacular.

A class that my wife and I were teaching at our church, which had prompted tremendous initial response—a packed room, in fact—

rapidly dwindled down to just a few people within a matter of weeks. A well-attended men's discipleship group that I had been leading for quite some time suddenly tanked, and every single person involved with it stopped attending. Then, on top of all of this, an event happened that shook my sense of calling and purpose to the core. I can't go into detail about what it was due to the fact that I would betray some confidences by doing so, but suffice it to say that this event made me question whether anything I was doing was producing anything good. I looked at all of the effort I had been putting into these various ministries and investing in the lives of others, and I saw very little results (along with some spectacular failures) in exchange for a considerable amount of effort. At that point, I was deeply discouraged.

It is fair to say that, at this juncture, my wife and I were burned out on church ministry.

The ship of my calling was adrift, in my mind, without any direction. Over the subsequent years, I eventually identified some of the missteps I had made that had contributed to some of the failures I'd experienced, but the discouragement I felt at the time left me at a loss about what to do next.

Looking back, I believe that God had strategically maneuvered me into a place where He could finally teach me the principles and beliefs concerning calling and purpose which I am about to reveal to you in the coming chapters. However, it was to take me five more years of sometimes painful learning and un-learning to get to the point where I finally realized my own true calling and arrived at a place where I could help others do the same.

Shortly after my ministry life hit bottom, we ended up moving to a new town, hundreds of miles away. When we arrived, one of the first items on the agenda was to find a church to attend. We visited nine different churches before finally locating one that we felt we could call home. By the time the dust settled from our having moved, finding a new church, getting kids settled in a new school, et cetera, I had come to a conclusion about my own personal calling—I had no clue what God really wanted me to do with my life.

Finding my way

I was burned out and clueless at this point in my journey. I still believed God had a specific plan for me, but I didn't understand what it was. I began to reflect on my past, and came to the conclusion that perhaps I had not taken enough time to wait on God. Maybe I had just been running off from one thing to the next, thinking that I had finally uncovered the coveted direction I was to take in life without really perceiving the truth. Maybe what I needed was to slow down and resist my natural urge to pursue the next big thing.

So, I decided to wait.

I made a commitment that, for the next year, I wouldn't join any church ministry, and I wouldn't try to personally 'fill in the blank' concerning what my individual calling or purpose might be. I would go to church and keep up with my own personal devotional life, and all that entailed, but I wouldn't try to define for myself whatever it was that God had created me to do. Instead, I would spend time in prayer and wait for God to show up and tell me what my calling was in whatever way He wanted to do so.

That first year was hard. I felt such a strong pull to jump into the next ministry, to fill in the blank, to busy myself and just do something, but I stuck with my determination to wait. Through that entire first year, I didn't hear anything concrete from God on what my calling was, and no concrete ideas begin to form in my mind about what it might be. There was a question that did begin to form in my mind: What will I do if God never tells me what my calling is?

As one year stretched into two, this question came to the forefront of my mind. As it did so, I began to re-examine what I had believed for so long about how calling and purpose are revealed and what the Bible actually teaches about these things. As time went on, I began to ask other questions. One of them was why is it so hard to hear from God in prayer? I mean, if God is real, all-powerful, and all-knowing, couldn't He come up with a more reliable form of communication? How about an email service, for instance? Why not just drop me a line and make it abundantly clear what my calling is in a concise email and be done with it? Why all the drama? Why must some of us go through such a torturous, uncertain, drawn-out process on the way to finding our true callings?

Eventually, a more alarming question began to pop up in my mind. If God might not tell me what my calling was, then what if I *never* found out at all? I had always assumed I would. It was, in my mind, a given that I would. But I was in my mid-forties and still hadn't grasped what it was. How long was this supposed to take, for Pete's sake? Intrinsically, I felt that if I was to find the level of fulfillment in life that I desired to have, then it was essential that I be pursuing God's intended purpose for me as an individual. The thought that God might not ever tell me what that purpose was—or the more likely scenario, that I would not hear Him correctly—was terrifying.

Humorous as some of the questions I was asking might be, I was actually beginning the process of deconstructing my long-held beliefs about calling and purpose, and asking the questions that needed to be asked. The answers to the questions came slowly, with some missteps along the way. It wasn't pretty, or neat, or well-planned on my part. But over the span of five years, I completed an important journey. I started from a place where false beliefs and an imperfect understanding of calling and purpose kept the carrot on the end of the stick always just out of my reach. I ended up in a place where I am now absolutely secure and content in the knowledge of what my personal calling is.

For me, the puzzle pieces finally fit. I've discovered what I was meant to do with my life, and I'm enjoying a greater level of personal fulfillment, peace, and contentment than ever before. The remainder of this book reveals what I learned during my journey, and reveals the steps by which you can take a similar path in order to discover your own uniquely personal calling in life. I firmly believe that if you follow the steps outlined in this book, then you, too, can enjoy the fulfillment that only comes from knowing and pursuing your God-given purpose with your whole heart.

Chapter 3 - Learning How to Be Still

As I began a season of backing off from the many ministry involvements that had characterized my life for decades, I started to feel uncomfortable. I almost immediately felt the desire to jump back into some ministry, even though I still had no idea what my personal calling was. But I had made a commitment to unplug for a year in order to really seek guidance from God about what He wanted me to be doing, rather than just go with what I felt, so I resisted this desire to fall back into my old pattern.

As this uncomfortable feeling persisted, I began to perceive what it really was. I began to understand that the motivation behind this uncomfortable feeling was a desire to pursue and receive God's acceptance. I was, frankly, a bit surprised by this revelation. I was, after all, a Christian. Theologically, I believed that Jesus' sacrifice of His own life on the cross in payment for my sins had made me acceptable in God's sight, and that nothing I could ever do or be would increase or add to the level of acceptance that I already had. But what I came to realize as time went on was that, while I believed this in my head, I didn't completely believe it in my heart. In my heart, I was still seeking God's approval, and I thought that if I was busy doing what I was called to do, then I would earn that approval which I was so desperately seeking.

As I began to discover the truth about my need to earn God's approval instead of peacefully enjoying this season of waiting, I started to see how this motivation had tainted my life in so many ways in the past. I began to see how my pursuit of a calling was not motivated solely by a pure desire to please God and fulfill my God-given purpose in life, but it was also motivated by this desperate desire for God's approval.

As I remained committed to the process of stillness and waiting on God, I slowly began to detoxify from this self-defeating motivation. I began to meditate on the good news message of salvation through Christ Jesus and really let it sink in that I didn't need to do anything else in my entire life in order to earn God's approval or acceptance. As time went on, I began to learn to enjoy simply being a child of God, without adding any works of ministry into the mix. I began to learn to enjoy my relationship with God again.

While I was going through this process of revelation regarding my own motives for pursuing a calling, I was continuing to struggle with the question I mentioned in the previous chapter. What would I do with my life if God never told me what my calling was?

Up to that point in my life, I had never really considered that I might not find my calling at all. It had been an accepted fact that I would. It was simply a matter of time and remaining dedicated to the task of doing my part by using my gifts as I was aware of them, seeking God in prayer, and waiting for God to move. But, now, I'd begun to doubt that certainty.

As time went on, I slowly became more comfortable with just being a child of God, apart from the acts of service and performance that had characterized my past. It was in this environment, where I had temporarily taken a break from any ministry commitments, that I began to ask a third question. What do I do while I'm waiting on God to reveal my calling – if He ever does? This question and others like it became my frequent companions during this season of waiting.

In the absence of the pressure I had previously put on myself to identify my calling, this latest question was relatively pressure-free. It wasn't a question that required me to plumb the depths of the mind of God or discern some mysterious message that God might be trying to communicate to me through various means. This question, at least in my mind, was much easier to consider.

The answer I arrived at, at least in the short term, was that I would write a novel.

I have been a writer since I was old enough to put words on paper. From those earliest days of writing sermon outlines as a child, I graduated to writing pamphlets and essays on Christian living. On one previous occasion, I had begun to write a rough draft of a novel, but I'd eventually abandoned the project and moved on with other things in my life. But now, as I was waiting around to see what God was going to do, I began to feel drawn to write.

It seemed like a fun idea at the time, to finally be able to say that I had written a novel. It would be something I could check off of my bucket list, if nothing more. So, I decided to go for it. Slowly, over a period of many months, I wrote my first novel, and in 2015, I self-published *Utopian Day* under the pen name of C.L. Wells. Though I didn't realize it at the time, this was to become an important milestone in my journey, as you'll see in coming chapters.

Everything I've discussed in this chapter was happening in a big, jumbled, non-sequential fashion—at least in my mind. I was wrestling with the aforementioned questions and attempting to write the next great American novel all at the same time. And life was moving on. Work, family life, et cetera. It wasn't a nice, sequential series of events where one revelation or experience neatly concluded before the next would begin. Frankly, it felt like I was wandering in the wilderness with only the slightest perception of any sort of plan.

In my mind, for the first two years (2013 - 2014), I was mainly waiting on God to do something with my mess, to answer my questions, and to essentially clear everything up and set me on course with my destiny. During this time, I was re-evaluating what I had come to believe about what a calling is, how God communicates with us, and what the Bible actually teaches about calling and purpose—as opposed to what I had believed for most of my life. This was some heady stuff to consider. As I continued on this path, the foundations of some of my false beliefs began to erode, and some new thoughts and possibilities began to arise in my mind.

As I really meditated on what the Bible teaches about calling, I realized that, while I had always assumed that God would tell me what my calling was at some point, the Bible never indicates that's the case. Sure, the stories I mentioned previously are striking examples of when God DID tell certain people exactly what their calling was - but nowhere in those stories does the Bible say that God will do this for everyone.

This concerned me a great deal. I was still in a place where I had some performance-based motivations. I still felt the pull to try and earn God's acceptance by working hard at whatever my calling might be. But if God wasn't going to reveal my calling to me, how was I going to earn that acceptance? Frankly, I was pretty anxious about the whole thing, but I was also tired, worn out, and ready for change. I was finally ready to begin confronting the truth. And the truth was, that for all of my Bible study, for all of the scriptures that refer to calling and purpose in the Bible, I simply could not find any Biblical support for the belief that God promised to reveal to everyone what their individual calling was in life.

(Pause for dramatic effect....)

This revelation, when it finally sank in, was a game-changer. I didn't come to this conclusion quickly, of course, but only after much meditation on the scriptures and pondering about what some of my favorite scriptures on calling and purpose in the Bible actually meant. As this truth began to sink into my mind and heart, other questions became more pressing. For, if God didn't promise to reveal everyone's calling to them, then I might be one of the people that didn't ever get that great email from the sky. And if God didn't reveal my calling to me, what was I going to do? How was I going to live the rest of my life?

One aspect of my life up to that point in time, which I haven't yet discussed with you, is that I had dealt with depression off and on for years. In hindsight, I now believe that much of that depression had to do with how my identity and self-worth were so wrapped up in this thing we refer to as 'calling' or 'purpose'. For most of my life, I'd been unsure what my calling and purpose were, even though many people around me would never have guessed that because of the confidence I displayed on the surface. I had even succeeded in fooling myself. As my real motivations and beliefs slowly began to be revealed, however, I began the process of learning the truth.

But I had not yet been set free.

Chapter 4 - Re-learning the Truth

If we could believe that we have great intrinsic value and worth, and be motivated only by a desire to make the world a better place by utilizing our gifts, talents, and abilities, then discerning and living out our God-given calling would be easy.

The truths contained in the above statement help to form the foundation of a clear understanding of calling and purpose. However, I didn't yet fully understand these truths at this point in my story. I was on my way, but I had not yet thought, prayed, and studied my way through some important questions that needed to be answered.

I was becoming increasingly concerned that there was a high probability that God might never tell me what my unique calling in life was. I reasoned that, if God had not yet revealed to me my calling in life by the time I was over 45 years of age, then I had probably already lived more than half of my life without discovering my calling. There was nothing I had found in scripture, nor in my personal experience, that gave me a high degree of confidence that God would reveal my calling in the second half of my life. True, Abraham was 75 and Moses was 80 when they received their respective callings from God, so it wasn't outside the realm of possibility that it just wasn't my time to find out yet. However, while a late-life calling reveal could be in the works, I still had a significant problem—what should I do in the meantime?

I had already spent around two years learning to rest and be comfortable with the fact that I could simply be a child of God without any other accolades or accomplishments, and that God would still love and accept me just as much as He ever would. However, as the motivation of needing to earn God's acceptance began to fade, the desire to discover and be about the business of living out my calling didn't. And why should it? One of the very first things God did when He created humankind was to give them a specific purpose - a goal to pursue. "And the Lord God took the man, and put him into the garden of Eden to dress it and to keep it." - Genesis 2:15. The first person's unique calling was to be a gardener!

Adam - the first man - was called to live in relationship with God, just like every human being ever born since. That is the first and greatest calling of all. But we aren't called to do this as robotic automatons that have no personality or free will. We are called to do this in the context of our unique individuality, given to us by God, and we are called to do this in the context of our individual calling and purpose. God is the Creator, and we are made in His image. We, too, are designed to create. Our calling is the God-given direction that we were designed to pursue with that creative ability, and we aren't designed to be content in life unless we are living that calling out.

So, without yet knowing what my calling was, I existed in this weird kind of limbo. I was increasingly at peace with simply being a child of God, yet I still felt this urge to find a calling—something to do with this creative passion that was stirring in my soul that would help give my life greater purpose and fulfillment.

It was during this time that I turned my attention to one of Jesus' parables, which was to play a pivotal role in my understanding of how God looks at calling and purpose. It was the parable of the talents in Matthew 25:14-30. In chapter 25 of Matthew, Jesus tells various stories that illustrate what the kingdom of God is like. In the parable of the talents, a rich man is traveling to a far country and gives a portion of his wealth to a few servants in order for them to manage it while he is gone. The word 'talents' here refers to an amount of money. The rich man returns some time later and takes an account of each of the three servants. Two have taken what the rich man entrusted to them and produced an increase. These two servants are commended. The third servant was afraid and buried the rich man's money in the ground when he first received it. Upon the master's return, this servant simply gave back the original amount. This servant was punished for his failure to invest what he was entrusted with.

I had often considered this passage in regards to calling and purpose, as it is frequently used in teachings and sermons on the topic. But in the light of my own personal journey of discovery, I now began to look at it in a new light.

In all the years I had been familiar with this story, I had never observed the fact that the rich man in the story never told his servants what to do with the money that he entrusted to them. It was evident that he wanted them to use the money in a way that would produce an increase in his own wealth, but he wasn't specific about the activities that each was to pursue in order to make that happen. Furthermore, the story relates that the rich man had given them each a different amount of money *according to their own abilities.*

A radical question began to circle around in my head. What if God's reason for not telling me specifically what to do with the gifts, talents, and abilities that He had given me was that He expected me to participate in the process of making that decision? What if God wanted me to help make the choice of what my calling would be?

At first, this possibility was a troubling proposition. What if I made the wrong choice? What if I couldn't decide at all? After all, when God visits you in the form of a burning bush and tells you to go to Egypt and deliver the Israelites from bondage, you may be scared to death, but one thing you are not is uncertain about what God is asking you to do.

But as I began to meditate on this question, I slowly transitioned from a place of fear to a place where this concept began to excite me. I had begun this journey at a place where my value and worth had been so tied up in this thing we call 'calling', or 'purpose', that I'd been terrified of not knowing or not succeeding at what it was. But I had moved on. My mindset had changed, and I had been marinating in God's unconditional love, independent of my performance or what I produced by my own efforts. And, in that place, this question became liberating.

As I studied and prayed and pondered the message of this parable in the light of everything else God had been teaching me, I began to change how I looked at calling and purpose. I began to transition from a place of looking at the process of identifying my calling as a stress-inducing roadblock in my life, moving on to a new paradigm where God was a loving Father Who had given His beloved child a set of building blocks in the form of gifts and talents, and was smiling as He stood back to see what His kid was going to build with them. I went from stressed-out and fearful to being liberated, confident, and excited!

With this change of mindset, I began to ask a new set of questions that ultimately led me to identify my calling in life. Questions like, 'If I could name my own calling in life, what would it be?' and, 'Given my own unique gifts, talents, and abilities, what do I find myself *wanting* to do with them?'

Once I began asking these questions in earnest, it didn't take me long to identify what I wanted my calling to be. I mentioned earlier that I had written a novel during this time of waiting. I had enjoyed the process immensely and I'd felt fulfilled in using my creative abilities toward that end. What I didn't mention was that there was an aspect of my writing that was intricately tied to my faith in God. I had wanted to write a novel for a secular audience, not one which was overtly Christian, but which presented God in a favorable light, where the Christian characters were good, strong, moral people instead of being the weak, ignorant, bigoted people that secular fiction often presents them to be. I'd wanted to write engaging and entertaining fiction that pointed people to God without being preachy, and which didn't contain the all-too-common, expletive-laden sex-fest that is rampant in much of secular fiction.

As I contemplated the possibility that writing could be my calling, I felt all the pieces of the puzzle beginning to fall into place. In the years that followed, I continued to write other works of fiction as well as non-fiction, and I experienced a growing sense of peace and contentment about my life that I had never really had before. Before—as previously detailed—although I'd been at peace with knowing I was a child of God, I'd remained anxious about the whole 'calling' thing. But that anxiety was slowly replaced with peace, and I began thinking of ways that I could use my writing talent to make the world a better place and help build the kingdom of God.

This new peace and contentment didn't develop overnight. Once I had identified my own calling, I found that I began to pursue it in much the same way that I had pursued things in the past which I'd thought might be my calling. For a while, I felt I needed to achieve a certain level of notoriety or income or number of sales from my writing in order to prove I was successfully living out my calling. I began comparing myself to other writers as a method of measuring my own efforts and success. However, over time, I worked through these issues and realized that whether or not I was a success at living out my calling couldn't be determined in that way. The more certain I became that I was doing the thing I'd been made to do, the less important the worldly markers of success in the writing field became.

I still work hard at my craft and seek to sell books and grow my audience, but it's no longer because I need that validation to prove that I'm doing what I'm called to do or to confirm that I'm a success. I can honestly say that my level of contentment with my calling has never been higher, and I'm excited about what the future holds as I continue to invest the gifts and talents that God has given me.

Once I had completed my own journey of discovery and identified my own calling, I began to get a vision for helping others do the same. Why should others be forced to figure this whole thing out on their own when I could help them by sharing the insights and lessons that I had learned in my own journey?

That was when I began taking notes and preparing to write this book.

I firmly believe that God orchestrated my journey. While I was doubting and frustrated and feeling lost, God was gently leading me through the events of my life to a place where I'd be able to receive the truth and finally believe it. I had to go through what I did in order to really internalize the truths that I needed to understand so that I could be set free.

Like me, you were also created for a unique purpose that only you can fulfill at this time and place in history. I'm honored and excited to help you in the process of identifying exactly what your unique purpose is, so that you, too, can find the fulfillment in life that God designed you to experience as you bless the world by living out your calling.

Chapter 5 - How to Streamline Your Journey

I've learned a few things by looking back over my own journey that can help make the trek along this winding path a bit shorter for my fellow travelers. I started out with no clue and fumbled through the process, making quite a few mistakes along the way. These mistakes delayed me from discovering my calling for years. Now that I've taken a hard look at what I went through and what I learned, I believe I have identified a process that you can follow to significantly reduce the time you might otherwise spend in the weeds, trying to find your way back to where you inadvertently strayed from the quickest route to your destination.

Whenever anyone takes a journey, it is best to pack appropriately. You wouldn't go hiking in the Alps without taking your trusty hiking boots and, ideally, a map and compass. Neither would you likely go to spend time at the beach at the height of the summer season without your swimsuit and some sunscreen. Similarly, this spiritual and intellectual journey you are on will be more enjoyable and successful if you pack the right stuff to take along with you. Consider the following as suggested gear for your journey.

Suggestion #1: Know thyself.

The first thing I would suggest that you do as you prepare to take this journey is to take some time and think about what you currently believe in your heart of hearts about calling. What do you think finding your calling is supposed to look like? How is it supposed to happen? How should a person go about discerning what their calling in life actually is? Do you even believe every person has a unique calling? Get a notebook, fire up the laptop, use your phone, or make a video—use whatever method you feel most comfortable with—but begin to chronicle your answers to these questions.

You might be clueless about how to even begin to discern what your calling is at this point. You might be thinking, "If I knew how a person should go about finding their calling, I wouldn't be reading this book right now, so how can I answer these questions?!" But the truth is that you *do* have beliefs about what a calling is and how a person discovers their calling. How do I know? Because people who are in search of their calling don't just jump out of bed one morning and decide they want to pursue some undefinable thing. You have some idea—even if it is a rather vague one—about what a calling is and what you are searching for. If you don't have any better idea than that, that's fine; start there and record it in your journal. By doing this, you're taking and important step to *own your beliefs*.

As you progress, I suggest you also write about how it feels to NOT know what your calling is. That can then inform what it is that you are really looking for. Do you feel like you don't know why you are here on planet Earth? Do you feel like you are just taking up space with no purpose, or that your life is largely unfulfilling? It's important to get past what you feel is the 'correct' spiritual answer and drill down to what you really feel. Of course, if you are a Christian, you know in your head that your life has purpose and meaning, but without knowing your calling, it's likely that you *feel* something quite different. It is quite possible that you are bored to tears with your life and feel that something significant is missing. Wherever you are in the broad range of possible beliefs, thoughts, and feelings on this topic, start recording these things. You will likely find that, as you do so, you'll discover you have more to say on the topic than you originally believed you would.

As you record your thoughts and feelings, I want you to skip the white-washed version that you would tell someone else. I want you to write down the unvarnished, raw, 100% truth about what you really feel and believe. This is your private journal—you don't have to share this with anyone else, so you can be completely honest. Do you believe God plays favorites, telling those He loves most what their calling is while leaving you out in the cold? Do you believe you just need to be more holy or pray more or fast for two weeks in order to reach a spiritual state where you are ready to hear from God what your calling is? Do you believe, as I did, that if you'll only work hard enough at doing what you think will please God, then one day he will make your calling clear by giving you astounding and obvious success, thus erasing all of your doubts? Do you wonder if you have a special, unique calling at all? Do you believe it should be easy to discover your calling and that hard work shouldn't be required? Do you believe that it will be effortless to find success once you finally discover what your calling is?

Whatever your questions, doubts, feelings, and beliefs are concerning calling in general, and as they specifically relate to you, document these things using your method of choice. The more in tune you are with your own personal beliefs and emotions, the easier it will be for you to spot the lies you have come to believe and change your false beliefs so that you can finally settle the issue of calling in your life and move forward.

I encourage you to continue this practice throughout your journey. As your beliefs begin to change, so will your emotions. Don't brush off or ignore your feelings—they're important indicators. While I don't recommend making major life decisions based solely on emotions, I would suggest that if you make big decisions in life while *ignoring* your emotions, then you can quite frequently end up making big mistakes. One of the reasons God gave us emotions is so they can serve as a flashing warning light that we need to dig deeper and find out where the emotions are coming from. Drill down to find the belief that is being hinted at by the emotions you're experiencing, and you can learn valuable information that can help you discern truth and uncover lies in your own life.

Suggestion #2: Give yourself some grace.

Taking this journey requires facing some hard truths about yourself. You have most likely believed some things that have held you back and sent you on some detours. Determine right now that you will give yourself some grace and forgive yourself for any mistakes you have made so far or that you will make in the future as you work through this process. Remember, you are a child of God, deeply loved by your Father. He doesn't despise you for not yet having figured this out. He is on your side and has guided you to this book to help you – I firmly believe that.

Suggestion #3: Don't take yourself so seriously.

I'll delve into this in more detail later in the book, but it is a great point to have in mind as you begin. *Don't take yourself so seriously.* What does that mean? It means that you and I are not capable of screwing up so badly that God can't set things right and get us back on track again. It means that there is no barrier so big that it can prevent you from living out your calling for the rest of your life. Not age, not physical impediment, not other people or circumstances—nothing. It means that it isn't all up to you and me. We aren't the most important component in the equation. Neither of us is superman or superwoman, and we don't have to be—the pressure is off. It means you can (and should) RELAX.

Think of a kid who's learning to ride a bike. His dad is there the whole time—picking him up when he falls, running beside the bike while he learns to pedal so that he doesn't have a bad wreck, and giving him a push-off so he can get some momentum. If the kid isn't taking himself too seriously, then he can have fun. It isn't such a big deal when he falls, or wobbles, or can't start riding without a push the first ten times. But, suppose the kid believes that his dad won't love him as much anymore unless he learns to ride the bike, or that his dad will think he's a great, big, fat disappointment as a son unless he succeeds at this task. Now that same kid isn't having fun anymore. Now, every wobble or fall or mishap has the potential to upend his world. After all, his father's love and acceptance is on the line!

Go find a mirror somewhere and look yourself in the face. Now, repeat after me, "It's not that serious." *Really*. I encourage you to do it right now. It's important for you to internalize the fact that God will love you just the same no matter what. He isn't mad at you for taking too long to discover your calling. He isn't disappointed that you haven't single-handedly discovered the cure for cancer. He doesn't think you are a no-good do-nothing. The sooner you can let go of all of that negative baggage that has made a toxic soup of negativity and self-loathing out of the whole process of finding your calling, the sooner you will be free to see the truth, discover and embrace your calling, and find the fulfillment you've been seeking all these years.

Suggestion #4: Don't be in a hurry.

I remember in my college days, when I would be especially interested in the topic we were studying in a class, that I'd want to spend more time learning about it. I'd want to camp out, drill down, and really explore the area of study that had sparked my interest. But the class would be on a schedule with a pre-defined outline of the material that was to be covered, and only so much time could be given to each section in order to meet the requirements of the course. As a consequence, the teacher would move on to new material and so would I, letting the dictates of the course schedule rule the day. Fortunately for you, there is no deadline that you have to meet when you are attempting to discern your calling in life. And as you are working through the process of discovering your calling, my advice is that you resist the temptation to complete this step too quickly.

Take your time so that you can really internalize the lessons of each step in the process. It will benefit you greatly as you proceed on your journey.

The younger person reading this book may be chomping at the bit to finish the process so that they can decide what major to take in college or so that they can decide whether or not they want to go to college at all, or if they should instead pursue something entirely different. The adults who find themselves reading this book at mid-life may feel the pressure of time itself, feeling that they're getting started far too late in their own personal journey to be taking their time, wanting to hurry up so that they can spend the time they have left on planet Earth doing something significant, fulfilling, and personally satisfying. I understand both motivations. I've experienced both of these motivations in my own journey.

If you are in either of these places or have an entirely different motivation for feeling like you want to hurry up the process, my advice to you is still the same. Feel the emotions of wanting to hurry through the process, acknowledge the very real motivations behind the emotions—and write them down in your journal or record them using your method of choice. But, once you've done that, resolve that you will NOT yield to those emotions, and will instead *take your time.* I guarantee that you won't regret it.

Suggestion #5: Remember that God is at work guiding your steps. You are not in this alone.

If you have spent considerable time and effort attempting to identify what your calling in life is, there is a better than average chance that you are frustrated with God's apparent lack of clear communication about the process. After all, you don't yet know what your calling is, or you have doubts about what it is, and couldn't God just clear this whole thing up with some obvious, heavenly download of information via angel-gram, dream, vision, or email? The answer, of course, is yes. God could shorten your journey and do just that, but He hasn't yet—and for good reason, as we shall discuss later on in this book.

The temptation, in this case, is to assume that you are really on your own. You may be tempted to believe that, for whatever reason, God wants you to stumble around like a blind pig hunting for truffles in the dirt, perhaps discovering your calling before you die or perhaps not, but He's not going to help. That would be an incorrect assumption. If God is Who He says He is in the Bible, then we know that God is interested in our lives, has great plans for us, and is actively involved in guiding our steps. Here are just a few choice verses from scripture to help illustrate this point:

> *"For I know the plans I have for you," declares the LORD, "plans to prosper you and not to harm you, plans to give you hope and a future." (Jeremiah 29:11, NIV)*

> *Trust in the LORD with all your heart and lean not on your own understanding; in all your ways submit to him, and he will make your paths straight. (Proverbs 3:5-6, NIV)*

> *I took you from the ends of the earth, from its farthest corners I called you. I said, 'You are my servant'; I have chosen you and*

have not rejected you. So do not fear, for I am with you; do not be dismayed, for I am your God. I will strengthen you and help you; I will uphold you with my righteous right hand. (Isaiah 41:9-10, NIV)

So, you may ask, if all these things are true about God, then why don't you get it yet? Why don't you know or feel confident in your calling yet? Why don't you feel fulfilled in what you're doing in life? Those are questions that we'll address later in this book. For now, I encourage you to have faith that God is definitely at work in guiding your life, and that He has a purpose for not yet having clearly revealed to you what your calling is. The good news is that, by the time you finish the process outlined in this book, I believe you will know why God has chosen to work in this way as well as know what your own personal calling is—so, take heart!

Suggestion #6: Set aside your current beliefs about calling and purpose, approaching this journey with fresh eyes and a blank slate.

Your ability to follow this suggestion is predicated on the assumption that you know what you currently believe about calling and purpose. If you haven't spent time discovering what your beliefs are yet, go back and review suggestion #1. It's important to take the time to determine what it is that you currently believe before proceeding—and don't forget to record it using your method of choice. Once you've identified what your beliefs are, then, for the remainder of this book, I want you to pretend that you have never heard of calling and purpose before, and are learning about this topic for the first time.

As you proceed on this journey, you will no doubt be challenged to believe something that contradicts what you currently believe. In the spirit of the process, I challenge you not to wrestle with it, but instead to temporarily assume that what I am telling you is the truth. Embrace the new belief as your own, if only until you finish the book. At that point, once I have painted the entire picture for you, *then* take a critical eye and compare the whole picture to what the Bible says, to what your heart and experience have said, and to what you have believed in the past. I believe you will find that I haven't led you astray and that it all makes sense.

Why is this necessary? Well, it isn't—if you want to spend five years going through a process that could take you far less time! You see, we humans have a tendency to talk ourselves out of the truth, using the lies we currently believe as the tools to bury the truths we are confronted with. We don't know they are lies, of course, but that's the problem. We see it every day. There are two or more sides to every political battle. One of the two sides—and sometimes both—are holding on to some misconception, half-truth, or outright lie in order to support their position.

If you try to bludgeon each new seedling of truth that I present to you in the following pages with the lies you have believed from the past, then you will stunt your growth and delay the discovery of your true calling. I was slow to believe some of these truths myself, and it delayed me for years. I'm attempting to help you avoid a similar delay. Tell yourself you will, at the very least, assume that what I'm telling you *might* be true. Then, as I've said, once you finish the book and see the whole picture, you can stack up what I've presented and put it on trial using your best arguments. Once you have examined the evidence thoroughly, I believe that you will agree with the picture I've painted and be set free to enjoy and fulfill your own personal calling.

Suggestion #7: Give yourself permission to express your anger towards God, and then let it go.

This is a biggie. After all, we aren't supposed to be mad at God, right? It's a sin, isn't it? Yes, as a matter of fact, it *is* a sin. So, why am I suggesting you give yourself permission to be mad at God? Because, in all likelihood, you already *are* mad at God, and until you expose that festering mess to the light of day, that anger will warp your perception of the truths that you need to understand so that you can be set free to pursue your calling.

If you are mad at God but are pretending that you aren't, you are only fooling yourself. God already knows you are mad at Him, and He has already forgiven you for it. He isn't upset or falling off of His throne or throwing a hissy-fit because you dared to be mad at Him. He is compassionate, slow to anger, and has great mercy (Exodus 34:6). Admitting you are mad at God and giving yourself permission to talk about it with Him openly is the first step in getting rid of the anger and being delivered from the lies you have embraced which caused the anger in the first place.

Perhaps an example will help illustrate the point. Suppose you are a parent, and you have a young child. You promise to give the child some ice cream when they get home from school, but after they have done their homework. Your plan, which you don't explain to the child, is to take them to the store and let them pick out their favorite flavor. The child comes home, dutifully does their homework, and then rushes to the refrigerator, opens the freezer, and finds… no ice cream. They run to you, tears streaming down their face, and say, "You lied to me! You promised to give me ice cream when I finished my homework, and you didn't!" They are angry at a *perceived* breach of promise. They've assumed, from what you told them, that the ice cream would be readily available immediately after they completed the last mark on their homework.

Now, in this situation, do you as the parent blow up? Do you berate your young child for having made a mistake in logic? Do you yourself now become as angry at your child as they are at you? Not if you are behaving like a good parent, you don't. As a good parent, you'll likely understand that they made an incorrect assumption and then gently explain to them what the plan was. Having learned the truth, the child will likely calm down and then go to the store with you to pick out ice cream—hopefully, after they have apologized for their outburst.

God is a good father. He is waiting to help you when you come to Him and honestly admit that you're angry with Him and tell Him why you're angry. It isn't for His benefit that you express your anger directly to Him; it's for you. Only then can He help you understand the error in your thinking and help set you free with the truth.

In my own journey to finding my calling, I had many prayer sessions with God during which I told Him how angry I was at Him for being so obtuse about what my calling was. I harangued Him for not being more clear about this topic in the Bible and about many other related things. And, it was through those conversations that I was eventually able to blow off enough steam to calm down and begin to take a fresh look at the whole process. The results of those many conversations and the revelations that followed helped me move ahead and eventually discover my own calling, and they paved the way for this book to be written so that I could help others find their calling, too.

The important thing to understand here is that you shouldn't let that festering anger turn into bitterness, and thus cause you to decide to give up on finding your calling altogether. That's the alternative if anger remains buried and unacknowledged, and if you don't push through it and make your peace with God. That's why it is so important that you give yourself permission to be mad at God. But, as you work through your anger, continue to meditate on the Gospel. Remember that this same God you may be mad at is the same One Who died a horrible death on a criminal's cross so that you and I could live with Him for eternity. Would that God set you up to fail? Would He toy with you and lead you on for no reason? Is that God an untrustworthy guide? Of course not.

As you honestly air your grievances with the Almighty, I believe that, eventually, you will likely admit that your anger was based on lies and misperceptions. You will likewise hopefully confess to God that you were wrong to be angry with Him—and He will be just fine with that, because He loves you and knows you aren't perfect. That, after all, is why Christ Jesus had to come and die for us in the first place!

Letting go of our anger towards God doesn't mean we have all of the answers that we are seeking. It means that we have come to a place where we have decided that we can trust that God's intentions towards us are good and pure, and that we can trust Him with our unanswered questions. So, allow yourself to express your anger with God, and then let it go so that you can move on.

Chapter 6 - What Identity Is and Why It Matters

The very first step in finding your calling is to clarify exactly who you are. You need to answer the question, "What is my identity?" Identity affects your motivation, your perception of reality, and your understanding of what is or is not important. These things, in turn, directly affect your ability to discern your calling accurately.

Let's look at an example of how our identity can affect us.

Suppose you're in a crowded restaurant, and an announcement is made over the intercom that a serious accident has happened just down the street. They describe the make, model, and license plates of the cars involved, and then end the announcement. You don't recognize any of the vehicles described as belonging to anyone you know. You're mildly concerned, say a quick prayer for the safety and well-being of those involved, and go on with your meal.

Now, suppose a slightly different scenario plays out. You are in the same restaurant; the same announcement begins, but with one significant difference. One of the vehicles they describe has the same make, model, and license plate code of your daughter's car. In this case, your reaction is going to be significantly different than in the first scenario. You're probably going to call your daughter's cell phone immediately, and if you can't reach her, you'll likely get up and proceed to the crash site as fast as you can so that you can check and make sure she's okay.

In the first scenario, you identify as a concerned citizen who is interested in the well-being of another person who just had a car accident. In the second scenario, you identify as the father of the person whose car was just involved in an accident.

Identity changes everything.

In a related fashion, your perception and understanding of your own identity directly affect your ability to accurately perceive what your calling is as well as your motivation to fulfill that calling. Correctly perceiving what your calling is directly impacts the level of passion and effort you will apply in the pursuit of your calling, as well as your personal level of satisfaction and fulfillment in the process.

Let's examine this topic of identity through the lens of a well-known story from the Bible—that of Moses.

If you aren't familiar with Moses' story, here's a primer: The Egyptians enslaved the Hebrew people for hundreds of years. At some point, the king of Egypt (the Pharaoh) decided that there were so many of these slaves that they might rise up and revolt, so he wanted to thin their ranks. He ordered that all of the Hebrew baby boys be thrown into the Nile River, where they would promptly drown or possibly be eaten by the crocodiles. Moses' mother couldn't bear the thought of drowning her young son, so she put Moses in a floating basket and placed it in the Nile. Moses was discovered and adopted by Pharaoh's daughter, and then raised as a prince of Egypt.

One day, Moses saw an Egyptian mistreating a Hebrew slave (Moses having most likely learned he was a Hebrew by that point), and he killed the Egyptian. Because of his crime, he was forced to flee for his life into the desert, where he promptly became a lowly sheepherder. Forty years later, God would appear to Moses in the form of a burning bush and inform Moses that was being called by God to deliver the Hebrews from Egyptian bondage. Through many trials and tribulations, Moses then followed God's instructions and eventually succeeded in his calling to lead the Hebrews to freedom.

Now, as callings go, you can't get any more clear than that. In fact, many of you wouldn't be reading this book right now if you'd experienced such a clear revelation of your calling. However, the point I want to make is that Moses' understanding of who he was provided the foundation from which he was able to fulfill his calling. I submit to you that, without a firm understanding of his identity, Moses would not have successfully fulfilled that calling.

Let's suppose Moses had a different backstory. Let's suppose he wasn't a Hebrew, but was from some other people group. Suppose he hadn't grown up in Egypt, and he didn't know who the Hebrews were. Only to then have the God of the Hebrews show up to him in the form of a burning bush one day, and tell him that he'd been chosen to deliver the

Hebrews from bondage to the most powerful country in the region. What do you suppose his reaction might have been? Would it have been different? I'm betting it would have been.

I imagine that, if this non-Hebrew sheepherder from the land of Canaan, who had never been to Egypt, had encountered God in this way, his reaction might have been something like the following: "Why do I care about some group of people enslaved in Egypt? I'm a sheepherder, for goodness sake. And who are you? You're some kind of god, but are you as powerful as the gods of Egypt? Thanks, but no thanks."

But that's not how it played out. In fact, upon closer examination of the story in Exodus, chapter 3, we learn a great deal about how important identity is for the person being called—as well as the One doing the calling. One of the first things God does after appearing to Moses is identify Himself (Exodus 3:6 NASB):

> ***He said also, "I am the God of your father, the God of Abraham, the God of Isaac, and the God of Jacob." Then Moses hid his face, for he was afraid to look at God.***

God knows that identity is central to a person's calling. That's why the first thing He does when delivering a calling to Moses is establish precisely Who it is Who is issuing the call. We'll discuss this more at a later point in the book. For now, just understand that God thought this was important to clarify before giving Moses his own calling.

The next point I want to make is that, once God has done this and told Moses what He wants Moses to do, Moses' first question concerns identity (Exodus 3:10-11 NASB):

> *"Therefore, come now, and I will send you to Pharaoh, so that you may bring My people, the sons of Israel, out of Egypt."*
>
> *But Moses said to God, "Who am I, that I should go to Pharaoh, and that I should bring the sons of Israel out of Egypt?"*

Moses' first question isn't, "Okay, how do You expect me to do this thing?" Instead, the first thing Moses does is challenge the validity of God's calling for him based upon his own faulty understanding of his own identity. In that moment, Moses thinks he knows exactly who he is. He's asking God a rhetorical question. Moses thinks he is unqualified to take on the challenge of this calling because he is the disgraced former prince of Egypt who is wanted for murder, who already failed to deliver the Israelites the last time he tried forty years before. He's making an excuse for why he can't possibly be the right person to fulfill this particular calling. God, of course, knows this, and responds in a way that is designed to encourage Moses not to fear, but to have faith that he can, indeed, accomplish the task with God's help (verse 12):

> ***And He [God] said,***
> ***"Certainly I will be with you, and this shall be the sign to you that it is I who have sent you: when you have brought the people out of Egypt, you shall worship God at this mountain."***

What happens next is very interesting. Moses understands, at some fundamental level, this whole thing about identity being key to fulfilling a calling. Moses knows that if he is to succeed in getting the Hebrew people to follow him, he will need to convince his fellow

Hebrews of the identity of the One Who gave him the command to lead them out of bondage. So, Moses asks God to reveal His name (verses 13-15):

> *Then Moses said to God, "Behold, I am going to the sons of Israel, and I will say to them, 'The God of your fathers has sent me to you.' Now they may say to me, 'What is His name?' What shall I say to them?"*
>
> *God said to Moses, "I AM WHO I AM"; and He said, "Thus you shall say to the sons of Israel, 'I AM has sent me to you.'"*
>
> *God, furthermore, said to Moses, "Thus you shall say to the sons of Israel, 'The LORD, the God of your fathers, the God of Abraham, the God of Isaac, and*

the God of Jacob, has sent me to you.' This is My name forever, and this is My memorial-name to all generations."

After this, Moses continues to demonstrate his reticence about the whole mission and argues with God about his suitability for the task, but eventually, Moses gives in and undertakes this journey to fulfill his calling from God. The takeaway here is that having a proper understanding of our identity—and God's identity, as well—is key to fulfilling our calling.

This same truth is made evident in the temptation of Christ in the New Testament (Luke 4:2-13). When Satan tempts Jesus in order to stop Jesus from fulfilling His calling, Satan does so by challenging Jesus' understanding of His own identity in two of the three temptations.

Satan starts two of the three temptations with the words, "*If* You are the Son of God..."

Satan also understands that identity is key to calling, and he is at work in each of our lives to warp our view of who we are and Who God is so that we won't fulfill our callings. In many cases, unfortunately, he succeeds in accomplishing his evil task. In the next chapter, we'll focus on practical steps to help unravel our perceived identity, discard the lies we have believed about who we are and Who God is, and embrace the truth so that we can discern and live out our calling with maximum effectiveness and clarity. But, first, we need to lay the groundwork by completing our examination of identity.

So far, we've established that identity directly relates to motivation, and motivation directly impacts the pursuit (or lack thereof) of our calling. But let's dig deeper. What happens when we have a warped view of who we are?

What happens when we believe we know who we are when we really don't? How can that affect our calling?

There are two ways you can define a thing. One way is to attempt to define what a thing *is* – that is to say, you can describe the attributes and function of that thing so that someone can tell what it is when they come across it. For instance, you can define a red wagon by describing it as being red and having four small wheels, a square metal bed about a foot or so wide and three feet long, a handle extending in the front of it that's about two feet long, and so on. The second way to define a thing is to describe what it is *not*. For example, one way to describe love is by saying that one of love's characteristics is the absence of selfishness. With that in mind and to help refine our understanding of identity, we're going to take a look at what it looks like when we *do not* have a good understanding of our own identity as it relates to discerning and living out our calling.

The failure to properly understand your identity can lead to the misuse of your gifts, talents, and abilities by influencing you to:

- Pursue your calling as a means to define who you are.
- Pursue temporal success as a substitute for your calling or pursue your calling with an over-emphasis on temporal success and the applause of humanity.
- Pursue a decoy or false calling because it offers either high praise from a peer group or worldly fame and fortune.
- Pursue your calling out of a motivation that is less about making the world a better place

(a.k.a. building the kingdom of God) and more about helping you feel that you are loved, valued, and accepted by God.

- Become confused regarding what your true calling is, or fail to correctly identify your calling.

A person who is unsure of who they are, and therefore unsure about their personal value and worth, can easily spend their life in the pursuit of personal validation instead of fulfilling their true calling.

Understand this: The world needs you to live out your calling. If you don't, there is no plan 'B' for touching the lives of others in the way that God uniquely designed you to touch them. Those opportunities will be lost, and the world will be less like the kingdom of God as a result.

Pick some significant person in your life and think for a moment about how they have affected you. This person could be someone who inspired you or helped you in a significant way, or it could be someone who hurt you or did something terrible to you. Think of the impact made by that particular person on your life. Now, imagine that person didn't exist—ever. How would the world be different? How would your life be different? If you imagined one of your parents, whether or not they were good or bad parents, if they didn't exist, then you wouldn't even be here—that's a pretty big impact. If the person you thought of was a teacher who inspired you to finish school or accomplish something significant, then if they weren't around you might not have gone to college, or competed in that sports event, or done something else of significance.

Just like others have had an impact on you, your life has an impact on others. If you live out your calling, then you will have the greatest impact for good that you could possibly have in this life. Correctly understanding your true identity is key to helping you live out your calling.

Without a solid understanding of who you are, temporal success or acclaim can easily become the guidepost by which you judge what your calling is instead of allowing God to define your calling in His own way. In this case, temporal success or acclaim, in effect, *becomes* your god in your effort to confirm and establish your value and worth in the universe. And worldly acclaim is a fickle god, whose determination of your value and worth is unstable, constantly subject to change with the affections and whims of humanity.

With a proper understanding of identity and its importance, we can begin to recognize areas in our belief system that hint at a misunderstanding of our identity. In some ways, it's like the movie *Karate Kid*, where the master martial artist first has the young apprentice wax cars and paint a fence in very particular and seemingly confusing ways, but without telling him why. Eventually, the apprentice learns that the movements he's been practicing are the exact movements he needed to internalize in order to perform certain martial arts techniques. In the same way, having a mental idea of how a warped understanding of our identity can manifest itself in negative ways helps prepare us for the next step, which is where we begin to pinpoint some of these manifestations in our own lives.

Looking at others to see ourselves

Sometimes it's easier to see something in someone else than it is to see the same trait or characteristic in ourselves, so let's look at some examples of misunderstood identity. As we do so, keep in mind that a key point in understanding identity issues regards looking at how a person is seeking to establish their value or worth. If a person's identity and worth are not properly grounded with an understanding of the fact that God loves and accepts them unconditionally, then they will try to earn their value and worth in some other way.

Consider the following examples.

Sarah is a woman who pursues serial relationships with men as a substitute for the love she never received from her parents. She is looking to have her identity established, and to have a man tell her she is beautiful, valuable, and worth loving—all the things her parents never confirmed about her. Her identity is in limbo. Consequently, because she is not secure in her own value and worth, she seeks to have her identity validated by the men she pursues. When she begins a new relationship, she very quickly becomes clingy, practically throwing herself at her latest love interest in order to get their attention. She becomes obsessive, controlling, and jealous when anyone of the opposite sex pays attention to her new man. But, instead of leading to her happiness, the tactics she employs in her frantic attempts to establish her value and worth end up pushing away the target of her affections.

If you know or have heard of a woman like Sarah, you know something is wrong. You may refer to her as needy, desperate, or even a slut. But what's really going on is that she is trying desperately to obtain proof of her value and worth in the world—a core need we all have. And because she isn't secure in that identity, she is wasting time and energy in counter-productive efforts to fill the hole she perceives inside herself.

Let's consider another example.

Jeremy pursues his career with dogmatic obsession. He is always gunning for the next promotion and a bigger paycheck. He never seems satisfied, no matter how much money he makes or what he seems to accomplish. He always wants a bigger house, a more expensive car, and membership at the most exclusive clubs. His goal is to be the CEO in the corner office, the king of the hill. He also never seems to be happy, and he's a workaholic who is slowly destroying his closest relationships by continually prioritizing career concerns over his relationships with family and friends.

This is a classic picture of what a misunderstood identity looks like. Desperate to establish they are valuable, this type of person keeps score with money, power, possessions, and/or fame in an attempt to establish their worth in the universe. They can never stop pursuing these things because, if they do, they believe someone else may prove themselves more valuable or successful, thus threatening their position in the pecking order of life.

What about an example that isn't so obvious?

Shaniqua dedicates herself to a cause that will improve humanity. She selflessly expends her time, energy, and money in efforts to further this cause. Her commitment is impressive. Her passion is inspiring. And yet, there is a perspective that seems to be missing in her life. She isn't just trying to make the world a better place; she is obsessed with whatever cause it is she's currently supporting. She eats, breathes, and sleeps the cause. The only friends she seems to have are those who are engaged in supporting the same cause. If anyone leaves the cause, their friendship with Shaniqua is also lost because she won't have anything to do with them anymore. In effect, her identity is so wrapped up in the cause that she isn't able to separate her identity from the cause itself. The success or failure of the cause becomes a referendum on her value and worth as a human being—a common expression of misunderstood identity.

One last example.

Jane's family is important to her. There are three generations of dentists in her family, she's an only child, and she's been groomed to take over the family practice from her father. She dutifully pursues training as a dentist and eventually takes over the family business, but she's not happy. She feels a lack of contentment with her career, but continues to pursue dentistry because it means so much to her family. She never really had any idea of doing something else when she was growing up, so she just went along with it. Now, approaching mid-life, she feels stuck in a job she increasingly can't stand and doesn't know what to do about it.

Jane's identity is wrapped up in her family. Consequently, her value and worth have come from her place in the family—a place that could have been jeopardized if she hadn't conformed to the family's expectations of her. Consequently, she has never felt free to explore other opportunities that could result in her realizing her true calling and thus living a more fulfilled life.

You may have already begun to recognize some of the adverse effects of a misunderstood identity in your own life as you've read this chapter. If so, that's good news! That's the first step to getting rid of the lies you have believed about yourself so that you can move forward. If not, don't worry about it. Just familiarize yourself with the manifestations and see if you can identify these symptoms in the lives of others you may know. We'll discuss practical steps in the next chapter, and those steps will help you discover how these behaviors and beliefs may be manifesting in your own life, as well as how you can get free of them so that you'll be able to find your true calling.

Action step:

Take some time and record your observations about the insights you have gained from reading this chapter. If you're beginning to identify some of the negative manifestations of a misunderstood identity in your own life, record your thoughts on this topic. Now take some time and think of others you may know who have manifested signs of a misunderstood identity. Do you see any similarities between their misuse of their gifts, talents, and abilities and your own journey? If so, record your thoughts on this as well.

Chapter 7 - Re-learning and Clarifying Your Identity

At some points on your journey to find your calling, you may have felt that there were forces working against you, trying to prevent you from discovering whatever it is you are meant to do in life. In a very real sense, you're right. Unfortunately, for many of us, one of these opposing forces looks back at us from the mirror every morning. That's right… you and I can help stymie our own efforts to find our true calling. One significant way we do this is through the decisions we make regarding the commitments in our lives.

The truth is that many of the commitments we make to people, organizations, and activities are heavily influenced by our need to validate our identity. These commitments can, in turn, hinder us in two ways. First, the validation we receive from them—whether such validation is positive or negative—influences our perception and decision-making with regards to our calling. Secondly, these commitments can often serve to keep us so distracted and busy with life that we cannot achieve the level of inner stillness that is needed to discern our calling. Once these two hindrances are remedied and any lingering identity issues have been addressed, the remaining process of finding our true calling can then become an enjoyable experience.

We discussed in the previous chapter how a correct understanding of our identity is one of the keys to unlocking our true calling. We also looked at a number of examples of how we can misunderstand our calling or pursue a false calling when we allow our identity to be defined in ways other than what God intended. The unhealthy validation we receive from the various commitments in our lives is a major contributing factor to misunderstood identity. In this chapter, we're going to learn how to address unhealthy validation in a way that will allow God to correct our vision of ourselves and solidify our identity entirely in Him, where it belongs.

What is unhealthy validation?

It's important to note that the validation we receive in our lives is not necessarily unhealthy in and of itself. Often, it is the way we internalize the validation that makes it unhealthy. For instance, if we help teach a Sunday-school class at church and we receive positive feedback from those who attend, and possibly from the pastor, this validation is not unhealthy in and of itself. But what if, in our heart of hearts, we believe we need to keep doing good works in order to earn God's love? We may never say it out loud, we may not even believe in our mind that it is true, but what if that's what we feel in our heart? If so, then the validation we are receiving from teaching the class can ultimately be unhealthy for us because the way we are processing it is unhealthy. We can be using it as proof that we've 'earned' God's approval through our service. In this scenario, the affirmation we are receiving is actually serving as an anesthesia to mask our own misguided understanding of God's unconditional love. In essence, the validation is helping to reinforce an inaccurate and ultimately harmful view of our identity. This can, in turn, be hindering our ability to discern our calling.

Another example of unhealthy validation would be if a parent or significant mentor constantly reinforces a certain career path or vocation, telling you that it is either your duty or your purpose in life to pursue it. Your desire to please this person—combined with the constant reinforcement they provide in implying that your value and worth are tied to your pursuit of the path they are encouraging you to pursue—can be a powerful motivator. It can also be unhealthy validation which keeps you pursuing someone else's idea of what your calling should be while simultaneously suppressing the true calling that was imprinted on your soul by your Creator.

In his autobiography, *Open*, Andre Agassi describes his own experience with this phenomenon. For those who don't know, Andre Agassi is one of the greatest tennis players of all time. From the time he was old enough to hold a racket, he was groomed by his father to be the number-one tennis player in the world—a goal that young Andre knew wasn't his own. In fact, the opposite was true. Listen to how Andre describes the feeling he had as he was forced by his father to spend countless hours practicing tennis when he was only seven years old:

> *I hate tennis, hate it with all my heart, and still I keep playing, keep hitting all morning, and all afternoon, because I have no choice. No matter how much I want to stop, I don't. I keep begging myself to stop, and I keep playing, and this gap, this contradiction between what I want to do and what I actually do, feesl like the core of my life. (Open, Chapter 1)*

Andre went on to spend decades of his life striving to achieve the dream his father had forced upon him. He earned millions of dollars doing so, but, by his own admission, he hated the game that consumed his life for so many years.

While this is a very clear example of unhealthy validation—of someone pushing their version of a life calling on someone else—there are a multitude of far more subtle examples in many of our lives. Unhealthy validation can often come from a loving parent who is, in their own mind, simply encouraging their child. If not accompanied with the instruction that we all need concerning how to discern our own, unique calling, this encouragement can be just as destructive. Perhaps we look up to a parent and therefore aspire to their vocation, and they innocently encourage this, believing that to be our true desire. We can easily receive this validation as confirmation of our own value and worth, and then slip into the false belief that our value and worth are dependent upon pursuit of the same vocation as the beloved parent. Thus, we can begin our own journey pursuing a false calling that we believe to be our own. If we are ever to get free from this cycle of unhealthy validation, we must see it for what it is and face the truth.

At the same time that you are addressing unhealthy validation in your life, you will be creating an environment that is far less busy and distracted. This will allow you to better process the new thoughts and feelings that will arise as a result of the removal of unhealthy validation, as well as those unaddressed thoughts and feelings that have previously been buried under a mountain of commitments and busy-ness.

Many of us constantly run around performing unnecessary and demanding tasks so that we can get validation from others instead of learning to receive God's eternal and persistent love for us. What we desperately need is to internalize the reality that God's love for us is immutable and independent of our performance. I refer to this process as disconnecting so you can re-engage. We temporarily disconnect from commitments and dial back on some relationships in order to clarify our identity and achieve the calmness needed to re-engage with our true value and purpose.

The process will vary in length from person to person. Some people might be able to accomplish it in as little as three months; others may find they need six months or a year or more to complete it. As you plan to implement this step, I would suggest you start by planning for a six-month period, and then adjust as needed. Don't get hung up on how long it takes, and don't try to rush it. Just understand that when all is said and done, you will be equipped to discover your true calling.

Removing distractions and misleading validation

We all seek validation of our identity. It's a core need. Yet, most of us are completely unaware of how our pursuit of this validation affects the decisions we make. In order to clearly see how your own pursuit of validation is affecting your quest to find your calling, it is helpful—and I would even say ***necessary*** for most—to temporarily remove as many sources of un-healthy validation from your life as possible.

But how do you identify the sources of misleading and unhealthy validation? The answer is that you probably aren't in a position to be able to clearly see all of the sources of unhealthy validation in your life. Until your identity is firmly and completely centered in God's unconditional love and acceptance, it is likely impossible for you to perceive all of the ways you are erroneously seeking or receiving unhealthy validation from other people, organizations, activities, and accomplishments.

So, how do you pinpoint the thing you can't see?

To help solve this dilemma, consider the following analogy. Suppose you have a good relationship with a significant person in your life. They might be a close family member, a romantic interest, your spouse, or, perhaps, a friend. Now imagine that person has to go away suddenly for six months on a long trip, and they won't have the ability to communicate with you in any way until they return. No cell phone, no email, no video conferencing, not even a snail-mail letter. Within the space of a week you begin to have a sense of loss, you realize how much you actually rely on that person's advice, or perhaps how often you use them as a sounding board to help you think through life's challenges. As the weeks turn into months, the list of things you miss about this person grows. By the end of the sixth month, you have a keen understanding of exactly what you miss about the relationship. You now realize things about the relationship that you would not have been able to quantify prior to this person's absence.

In addressing the existence of unhealthy validation in our lives, we are going to use the same principle.

If you temporarily pause many of your non-essential commitments and limit certain types of interactions for a space of time, you will begin to have longings for the things you miss and, quite possibly, a deeper level of peace and calmness because of some of the negative influences that are now absent. These feelings and emotions will help point you in the direction you need to examine further for potentially unhealthy validation.

It's important to understand that this isn't a plan which most people can implement overnight—it takes some planning and forethought. It's also important to understand that this isn't a bridge-burning expedition. I'm not suggesting you neglect your familial responsibilities, quit your job, or cut off your friendships. This step is a means to an end. In order to find your true calling, you need to know the truth about yourself and why you do what you do. This process will help lead you to those answers. And once this step is completed, you can selectively add back into your life many of the things you removed, but with a healthier perspective. You will likely discover some things that need to be gone for good, as well—and that's okay, too.

To begin with, start making a list of all of the commitments you have in your life. On your favorite electronic device, or perhaps on a sheet of paper, on the left-hand side, begin listing the names of people to whom you have some regular commitment. You'll possibly list your spouse or significant other, children, parents, friends, et cetera. Next, begin listing organizational commitments. Your job should be listed here, along with your college or trade school, commitments at your church, et cetera. Finally, add any other regular recreational or extra-curricular commitments, as well as any other significant voluntary or involuntary commitments you have in your life that I may not have covered in the above description.

Next, on the right-hand side of the page, begin to list the specifics of what you are committed to in each of these cases. Don't get caught up in the details of every single thing you are committed to—as in a family relationship with a spouse, for instance. Instead, limit yourself to identifying those things that are not essential, that take up more than an hour of your time in a given month, and that are long-term. If you are committed to going hiking once a month with your spouse, then put that down. However, you wouldn't list the fact that you are committed to being faithful to the relationship because that is an essential aspect of your relationship. Instead, focus on the non-essential aspects of the relationship. For your job, which is likely an essential commitment, you'll only list things in the right-hand column if they are non-essential, job-related activities. Do you volunteer every year to help organize the company picnic? Put that down. Are you working sixty hours a week, well over the required amount to remain employed? Put that down.

It's important that you make a thorough list. If you help organize class birthday parties for your child's class at school, that would go on the list on the right, across from the 'children' category. Are you on the prayer team at church? That goes in the right-hand column across from 'church'. Are you on a tennis team that requires regular practice and game time? Put that down in the right-hand column across from 'recreational commitments'. When you are all said and done, your list might look something like the following:

People, organizations, and activities	Non-essential commitments
Spouse	Go hiking once a month
Children	Help out organizing class birthday parties at their school; personally drive them to soccer practice; PTA event committee member.
Work	Help organize annual picnic; work overtime on a regular basis.
Church	Prayer team; weekly fellowship group; church greeter; lead the middle-school Sunday school class.
School	Taking classes for a degree program at community college.
Recreation	Tennis team (weekly games and practice).

The commitments listed in the previous table would make for a very busy person, and it might seem exaggerated, but many people who under-take this exercise will be surprised to discover just how many non-essential commitments they have in their lives.

Don't rush this process. Take a couple of weeks to really make a thorough list. The more complete your list is, the better prepared you'll be to begin the next process: planning how to temporarily reduce your participation in non-essential commitments.

Some things to keep

I want to take a moment to discuss some non-essential commitments in your life that you should not completely remove from your life during the disconnection phase. Regular worship with fellow Christians, regular exercise, and those things you are doing which are part of normal, healthy self-care (like hobbies, family game night, and hanging out with friends) are some of these things.

It may take you some time to think through the distinction between what needs to be suspended temporarily and what you should keep doing, but take the time to pray and journal about it. Going to church once a week for fellowship and worship should still be a part of your life, while teaching the Sunday school class next quarter is a good candidate to put on the list of things to temporarily stop doing. Going out to lunch with friends is a good thing to keep on the list, whereas serving as team captain and organizing the softball season for the team you all play on every year would be a good item to move off of your plate.

Re-engaging with the truth

If all this process were designed to accomplish was to provide you with some alone time so that you could meditate and be free from unhealthy validation, it wouldn't be enough to prepare you to accurately discern your calling. An essential part of the process is what you do with the time you have once you have reduced the distractions and sources of unhealthy validation.

As the title of this chapter indicates, this process is designed to help you re-learn and clarify your identity. As you are moving through this process of removing sources of unhealthy validation and creating additional quiet, un-distracted space in your life, it is essential that you are meditating on the truth about your identity. Disconnection is all about removing, for a season, as many of the non-essential activities in our lives as is feasible, so that we can break free of the performance / unhealthy validation trap. Re-engaging is about internalizing the reality that BEING a child of God IS ENOUGH.

During this time, it is essential that you meditate on the good news about Jesus Christ on a regular basis. Now, most of us know the technical aspects of the good news—or the Gospel, as it has been traditionally called. Our sin separates us from God, and the results of that sin are spiritual and physical death, but Jesus died on the cross at Calvary after having lived the perfect, sinless life in order to pay the penalty for our sin. Now, if we will receive Him as Savior and Lord, we can experience eternal life with God forever, free from the burden of debt we owed due to our own sin. If you have never heard the good news before—there it is! You can read about this in the Bible in the following passages (among others): Romans

3:23, Romans 5:8, Romans 6:23, and Romans 10:9-10.

Many of us can remember a moment of decision when we chose to believe the Gospel and accept Jesus as our Lord and Savior. However, that doesn't mean that our minds were instantly and completely transformed, and that we began living in every area of our lives according to that reality. If you have made that commitment to Christ, you have found eternal life in Him. However, you can still be making decisions on a daily basis which are driven by an inner felt-need that you need to perform or achieve 'X' before you'll be truly valued and accepted by God or be fulfilled as a person. Romans 12:2 tells us that the transformation from living according to an un-godly mindset to a Christ-centered, truth-based mindset is a process that occurs as we renew our minds. This is a process that takes time and effort on our part if it is to be successful. The steps I'm outlining will help facilitate the renewal of your mind as it concerns your identity.

Below is a good summation of how a person thinks when they have internalized the truth of the Gospel. I suggest you write it on a 3 x 5 card, put it as the splash-screen on your computer or phone, or print it out and paste it on the refrigerator—put it wherever you will see it frequently during the day, and take the time to read it out loud to yourself frequently. There is something about reading it out loud that helps internalize the truth of it in our hearts. It is the way humans were designed to learn and to establish truth in our minds and hearts. When God creates, He SPEAKS a truth. We are created in God's image and have the power to do the same.

The Good News:

God's love for and
acceptance of me is not based on

temporal achievement or performance. Instead, God's love for me is based solely on the fact that I am His child. His love for and acceptance of me will NEVER CHANGE. He will never reject me or love me less because I have done something wrong or failed to meet some standard of performance. And He will never love or accept me more, regardless of how much my performance improves or how much I accomplish for His kingdom. God's love for me is unchanging, eternal, and forever settled. I am greatly loved and cherished by God just the way I am.

Now, I know someone out there is thinking, "But what we do *does* matter! We can't just go on sinning and think everything is okay between God and us!" And that's true, but the problem is that we often confuse sanctification with justification—two important spiritual concepts. Justification is the process of being made right or righteous, of being put in right standing in relation to a person or an entity. It is a state of being in which all obstacles to a good relationship between two parties have been removed. Our value and worth are based upon the fact that we are justified before God—which is a work of grace that is based solely on the free gift of God through Jesus Christ, and not on our personal performance or achievement. Sanctification, however, is the process of learning to live a life free from sin and is a life-long process that does require our participation and effort (i.e., our performance). The problem for most of us is thinking that we must be *sanctified* (meet Biblical performance standards)

BEFORE we can be *justified* (accepted and valued by God)—which is a lie.

Suppose a man has a five-year-old son. The father doesn't love his son because of anything the little boy has done. He loves the young boy simply because he is his son. It is not based upon the boy's performance but on the relationship the boy has with the father. This is similar to God's love for us. When Christ died on the cross for us, He made it possible for us to be adopted into God's family and become sons and daughters of God, making us eternally accepted by God because of Jesus' sacrifice and not because of our own performance. This is justification.

Now, suppose this father asks his son to clean off the table after dinner. The young boy does his best, but when he's done, the table still has specks of food on it. It doesn't meet the father's standards for a clean table. The father comes in and notices this. As a good father, he doesn't get angry and scold the son because his performance doesn't measure up. And why not? The boy has clearly failed to meet the standard set by his father (i.e., the boy is not sanctified). The father doesn't stop loving the boy simply because his performance isn't perfect. Why? Because his love for his son was never based on performance. His love for his son was based on the relationship that was established when the boy was born. He may ask his son to come back to the table and walk him through the process of wiping off the remaining crumbs, but it doesn't affect his love for his son one iota.

This is the reality we need to grasp to most effectively discern our calling. When we receive God's gift of forgiveness through Christ Jesus, we are born again and become God's own sons and daughters, and God's love and acceptance of us are part of our birthright—one that can never be lost simply because we leave some crumbs on the table.

Believe this. Meditate on this. Let this way of thinking soak into your soul. It will change your life.

We should all continually work with God's leading and enabling grace to turn away from sin, but we should always remember that His love and acceptance of us are never tied to our success in that pursuit. I don't love my kid more because they finally clean up their room like I've asked them to. When they do finally clean their room, it does help improve the *experience* in our relationship and the level of fellowship and closeness that we feel towards one another, but it never affects how much I love them.

The above truths are powerful, life-changing, and radical. As you begin to experience life without the crutches of performance or past commitments that have been feeding your felt-need for validation and worthiness, the truth of the Gospel will be a soothing balm to your soul. It is only as you internalize the truth about God's love for you that you can really begin to purge yourself of the false-need for human or material validation and replace it with God's genuine love and acceptance, becoming settled in the reality that BEING a child of God is ENOUGH.

Planning your disconnection period

Your next task is to make a plan for temporarily removing as many of the non-essential commitments in your life as is feasible. Begin by taking the list of commitments you created and examine each item listed in the right-hand column. For each distinct item listed, use your journaling method of choice and ask yourself four questions:

1) Why am I committed to this activity?
2) What do I get out of it?

3) How do I feel about my commitment to this activity?

4) How can I temporarily reduce or eliminate my commitment to this activity during my disconnection period?

Let's work through an easy example of how this might look, taking an item from our above list, and then move on to a more complex one. The way these questions are answered will look different for different people. I'm going to give two examples of how these questions might be answered for the activity, 'working overtime at work'. This first fictitious example is from Tara, who is married with two kids:

Example #1:

Activity: working over-time at work.

Why am I committed to this activity?

We have two car payments and a house payment in addition to other bills. We need the extra money so we can save a little and do some of the fun activities we like to do, such as eating out and saving for a vacation.

What do I get out of it?

I get to eat out at nice restaurants and go on a decent vacation.

How do I feel about my commitment to this activity?

Honestly, I'm glad I have the opportunity to work overtime, but I would really enjoy getting to spend that extra time with my spouse and kids. Sometimes I think we should find other ways to cut back so I won't need to work overtime so much.

How can I temporarily reduce or eliminate my commitment to this activity during the disconnection period?

I could discuss with my spouse the possibility of cutting back on or temporarily stopping overtime work during this planned disconnection period.

In the above example, we see that Tara is willingly trading the extra time spent at work for the opportunity to eat out at nice restaurants and go on a better vacation than she would otherwise be able to enjoy. The validation she is receiving doesn't appear to be related to her identity, i.e. her value or worth as a person. Instead, she seems to have made a very deliberate decision to be committed to the activity of working overtime in return for some very clear, tangible benefits.

While this activity doesn't seem to be providing any unhealthy validation in her life, it does require a significant commitment of time. Since we're also looking for ways to create space in our lives to allow for meditation, de-compression, and calm, it is one area to consider for reducing the busy-ness factor. If you are too busy, it will be much harder to achieve the clarity of mind and space required to discern your calling accurately.

Example #2:

Activity: working over-time at work.

In this example, John has a wife and child, and he's working overtime for a very different reason. Let's see how he answers these same questions:

Why am I committed to this activity?

With all of the projects I have at work, I just can't seem to keep them all on track unless I work long hours. My boss is continually pushing me to stay on schedule, but there never seems to be an end to the demand for me to do more.

What do I get out of it?

I get more projects done so my boss stays reasonably happy with me, and I get more money in my paycheck. Also, I want to get that next promotion, and if I don't get all these projects done on time, I'm afraid my boss will give the promotion to someone else.

How do I feel about my commitment to this activity?

I can't stand it. Some weeks, I'm working so much that I hardly have any time for me or my family after I get off work. Most days, all I have the energy for when I get home is to eat dinner, shower, and go to bed.

How can I temporarily reduce or eliminate my commitment to this activity during the disconnection period?

I need to seriously think about transferring to another area of the business where the demands on my time aren't so intense. I'm just not happy with this work environment and I'm ready to make a change for my long-term happiness.

For John, the choice to work overtime has some very different implications than in the first scenario. John appears to feel coerced into the situation rather than it being a voluntary choice which he wholeheartedly agreed to. The reason he gives for continuing to work the overtime is to please his boss in an effort to hopefully secure a future promotion. He is also experiencing some clearly negative effects of this choice, due to the long hours spent at work.

John is absolutely experiencing unhealthy validation. The boss is clearly indicating to him that his value and worth at the company are due to his completing as many projects as possible on schedule. Is this unhealthy validation hindering John's ability to discern his calling? Maybe. If John is basing part or all of his value as a person on his ability to earn money or excel in a career, then it could absolutely be hindering his ability to discern his true calling. Remember, we often can't accurately perceive the sources of unhealthy validation in our lives until we temporarily remove them.

John has a choice to make. He feels that he was created for something more in life, but he feels pressure to keep up with a demanding work schedule so that he doesn't lose the opportunity for a promotion at work. As a source of validation in his life, he also must consider the possibility that he's allowing his job performance to be an unhealthy source of identity. In addition to all this, the amount of time he's spending on overtime will negatively impact his ability to create the space and calm necessary to discern his calling.

It's a difficult decision to make. If John chooses to reduce the number of hours he spends at work, he will likely want to have a frank discussion with his boss and come to some sort of agreement on the maximum number of hours he's willing to work. Decisions like this must be made with care, as we all have financial commitments and most of us can't afford to lose our jobs. If John thinks he might get fired for pursuing this course of action, then part of his planning for the disconnection process might be to look for another job, or, as was mentioned above, possibly transfer to another department where there won't be so much demand for him to work overtime.

For the next example, let's look at the commitment to children's sports. Consider a parent who has signed their two young girls up for the soccer season. It requires two practices after school each week, plus a game on the weekend, which might require travel to another town. It's a huge time commitment. Let's take a look at how Joan (whose daughters are Jill and Sarah) might process this in her journal.

Example #3:

Activity: kid's soccer

Why am I committed to this activity?

The kids need exercise, and soccer is a team sport that will help develop skills they need to work with others. Also, Jill seems to love it.

What do I get out of it?

I get the satisfaction of knowing I'm doing something healthy and character-building for my kids.

How do I feel about my commitment to this activity?

I love seeing them play and have a good time with other girls their age. It is a huge time commitment, though, and sometimes I wonder if it would be better if we did something that didn't require us to be gone from home so much of the time. I feel like I'm constantly on the go.

How can I temporarily reduce or eliminate my commitment to this activity during the disconnection period?

I could ask my husband to take the kids to practice once a week so I don't have to, and discuss with the family the possibility that I might only attend the games every other week (hopefully my husband will agree to go solo on the weeks I miss).

Joan sounds as if she's committed to taking her kids to soccer for all of the right reasons. Her daughter Jill even seems to love the game. No problem here, right? Before I tackle that question, I want to acknowledge that commitments directly involving other family members are often complex and involve many different motivations and considerations. It's not always easy to discern our own emotions or motivations from a simple journaling exercise, and neither should we make a unilateral decision to end a commitment without considering the effects it will have on the others involved.

Now, back to that question. Is there a problem here? Possibly. If the time commitment Joan is making keeps her too distracted to achieve that place of inner calm required to discern her calling, then, yes, it's a problem. If Joan has a full-time job or other commitments that keep her busy all day, then she would certainly benefit from reducing her time commitment to the soccer effort. In addition to the ideas Joan mentioned above, another solution might be to have a discussion with the family in which they decide to skip a season of soccer all-together. There are many creative ways to reduce or eliminate the time spent on children's sports. For many people working through this process, it will be a necessary part of the disconnection process.

While we don't see any obvious signs of validation issues in Joan's response above, we need to consider that this commitment may also be providing unhealthy validation. Perhaps Joan's parents never let her play sports, and it was something she always wanted to do when she was growing up. Maybe she sees part of her success as a mother as being tied to providing her children with this opportunity. If so, then part of her value and worth as a mother comes from having provided her children with sports opportunities.

I think we would all agree that it's a good thing to provide your children with opportunities. However, if we feel we're a bad person if our kids don't play a sport, it can lead to a situation in which we might unknowingly coerce our children into a sport they actually don't enjoy, or put so much emphasis on them playing a sport that they themselves begin to feel our love for them is somehow conditioned upon them being involved in the sport that Mom or Dad seems obsessed with. If Joan is influenced by any of these motivations, she would benefit from taking a break from team sports for her kids, because it would assist her in facing her own related identity issues and remove a source of unhealthy validation.

It's relatively easy to identify areas of commitment in our lives that are non-essential. It's not as easy to identify which of these commitments we are unknowingly clinging to as a source for validating our self-worth or identity. If you are able to make the connection to how the commitments you have made in your life connect to your identity at this point, that's great. If not, don't worry. That clarity will come as you move forward in this process. At this point, by seeking to eliminate or greatly reduce the non-essential commitments in your life, you are paving the way for those revelations.

Once you complete the journaling exercise mentioned above, you will have the beginnings of a plan for implementing your own disconnection period. Take some time to review all of the answers you have compiled for question #4, "How can I temporarily reduce or eliminate my commitment to this activity during the disconnection period?" The answers you provided form an outline of what you can do to disconnect from unnecessary commitments and begin to expose sources of unhealthy validation in your life. Once you have reviewed these answers, set a target date by which you believe you can implement the steps you've outlined. That date will be your goal for beginning your planned disconnection period.

Remember that the date you set is just a target. For some of you, implementing the steps you outlined will take very little time. For others, it may take six months or more of planning and executing gradual steps before you can responsibly reduce your commitments enough to begin your disconnection period. How long it takes is less important than the fact that you are moving toward that goal. Your target date may change. That's normal. The important thing is that you set a target date and move toward that goal. Don't be discouraged if it takes longer to prepare than you expected. The very fact that you are planning and implementing the plan puts you one big step closer to your goal of discovering your true calling in life.

Overcoming fear so you can move forward

It is entirely possible that you are experiencing some level of anxiety at the thought of making all of the changes you've identified so that you can begin the disconnection phase. That's completely normal. For some of you, this amounts to making some drastic life changes that will completely alter, for a time, your lifestyle, and also affect many of your significant relationships.

I understand.

Years ago, when I was experiencing some marriage issues, I decided that I needed to cut back on the number of hours I worked every week so that I could be home more and make my marriage more of a priority. It wasn't an easy decision to make, but I decided that saving my marriage was more important than the temporary discomfort required to make the change. I ended up quitting my job in the city and taking a much lower-paying job near home. It was a big decision, and it came at the very tangible cost of reduced income, but it was the right thing to do for my marriage and I'm glad I did it.

You may think that you couldn't possibly make all of the changes I'm suggesting, but the truth is that you can. You just need to decide what's more important to you. Do you want to continue on the path that you're already on in hopes that it will one day lead you to fulfillment in life? Are you sure that it will? If you've made it this far in the book, then I think we both know that you need to make a change.

If you want to find your true calling and the fulfillment that comes from living it out, then perhaps you need to take the leap of faith I'm suggesting.

So, now what?

We've already discussed the goal of meditating frequently on the good news about Jesus Christ as you move through this process, but what else should you be doing during the disconnection phase?

For many of us, we have a mindset that busy-ness produces results. So, we jam our lives full of activities that are designed to produce a certain result—a more fit body, a better job, a happier kid, whatever. We've discussed the process of reducing many of these commitments and the logical question to ask is, what do we replace these commitments with? Besides meditating on the Gospel, the answer is, at least initially, nothing.

That's right. You read that correctly. I want you to do a whole lot of NOTHING. Now, I'm not suggesting you just stare at the walls or binge-watch that television series you've been planning on. Instead, I'm suggesting you only participate in activities that give you plenty of time to think and provide an opportunity to sit with your own thoughts. Take walks in the woods, ride your bike, visit the library, put a puzzle together, build a model ship, plant some flowers in the yard, maybe paint that room you've been putting off painting—anything that doesn't involve a long-term commitment and which allows your brain to think at the same time.

Why am I suggesting this? I'm suggesting this because many of us are getting our 'feel-goods', our sense of value and worth, from the things we are DOING. But our true value and worth don't come from DOING anything. A person's true value and worth come from BEING a child of God. And until we can stop mainlining the drug of temporal achievement long enough to detoxify from the addiction of human approval or material possessions, we cannot internalize and experience the truth that simply BEING a child of God is ENOUGH.

By taking the time to do NOTHING, you are giving yourself the gift of detoxification from many of the external validators that you've previously used to help prop up your identity and feelings of self-worth. You will likely, as I did, begin to feel uncomfortable. You may feel a need to DO something to erase these uncomfortable feelings. It is important that you resist this urge. Instead, use your journaling method of choice and begin to record your thoughts and feelings. Dig down deep. Whenever emotions surface during this time, start your journaling process by asking yourself two questions. First, ask yourself, "What am I feeling?" Are you bored, angry, sad, or frustrated? Whatever you may be feeling, record these emotions. Next, ask yourself, "Why do I feel this way?" You may need to go through several cycles of answering these questions, over days or even weeks, in order to get a clear picture of what your true feelings are and why you feel this way. Take your time. Your feelings are important, and they are valuable guides that will eventually lead you to the truth if you let them.

Your feelings and emotions are signposts. Some of the things your emotions can point to are the sources that you're using as validators of your identity. If there's some commitment which you've temporarily removed from your life that you feel compelled to add back in or replace with some similar pursuit or relationship, it is highly likely that you have just discovered something or someone from which you are receiving unhealthy validation. I'm not referring to something or someone that you simply miss, like how you might miss surfing at the beach back home when you're on a long trip to Montana. I'm talking about a feeling that your life is incomplete without that activity, that you are somehow without a purpose unless you are doing that thing. As you sit with these emotions and journal about them, while also answering the suggested questions above instead of trying to immediately satisfy the felt-need, the truth behind why you feel such a desire to jump back into the commitment will surface.

Through this process, you will likely discover that your motivations for doing something or spending time with someone are mixed. There are good reasons for many of the activities and commitments we make. If there weren't, we likely wouldn't have gotten involved in them in the first place. Taking the time to step back and sort through the emotions we have surrounding these decisions will help you sort through the good, the bad, and the ugly. At the end of the process, you will have a better understanding of all of your motivations for making the decisions you've made in the past. Armed with this knowledge, you will be empowered to make better, more informed decisions about what you want to keep in your life, and what you need to let go of in order to find your calling and experience greater fulfillment in life.

I've already mentioned that one of the things I discovered about myself when I went through this process was that the intense desire I felt to pursue certain goals was ultimately a desperate attempt to confirm my value and worth in the universe. I felt that if I wasn't doing something to build God's kingdom in others that I was failing to fulfill my purpose and was therefore failing to please God. I felt as if I was becoming a disappointment to Him—a lie which I desperately needed to be set free from. As I journaled, and waited, and meditated on the good news of God's love, I began to be healed from misconceptions like this. It is revelations like this that you will be discovering as you wait, meditate on the Gospel, and journal in the disconnection zone.

In the coming chapters, we'll discuss some other things that you'll want to slowly begin incorporating into your life during this phase. But one thing we want to avoid is simply exchanging the old commitments and activities for new ones. You need empty space and time in your life to reach the goal we're aiming for.

Let the process work

As you move into this time of disconnection and begin to meditate on the truth of the Gospel daily, it's important that you let the process work. Time itself is a crucial component of the process. You need to marinate in this state for quite some time before you can truly detoxify from years and years of functioning with an incorrect understanding of your identity. Don't think you're done in a month and try to move on. I suggest taking at least six months to hang out here. You'll be surprised to find that, just when you think you are finished, another layer of self-doubt and insecurity will pop up because of a situation you find yourself in. Then you'll have an opportunity to get an even deeper level of healing as you meditate on the Gospel and let God's love heal the freshly exposed wounds of the past. That only happens if you give the process time to work without being so distracted by commitments to DO stuff in order to earn your value.

I can't stress this enough. Jumping back up on the horse too quickly can short-circuit the process and leave the work of clarifying and solidifying your true identity half-finished. I took about two years to go through this process myself, and I was amazed that just when I thought I had settled my identity issues, something else would crop up and reveal that I still needed to internalize the truth of the Gospel at a deeper level. Some place in the basement of my soul still needed more healing. I'm glad I didn't stop too soon.

So, how do you tell when your time in the disconnection zone is over? Truthfully, the process of transformation that *begins* and is *established* during this time is never really completely over. If you so choose, you can continue to deepen your understanding of your identity for the rest of your life as you progressively apply these principles. However, for our purposes, deciding when to move on to the next step is something you have to determine between you and God. If you sense you need longer than six months, take it. I started out with the idea that I would take a year and ended up taking almost two years.

Don't be afraid of making the wrong decision here. Making the wrong decision isn't fatal. If you've taken the recommended six months and feel that you've worked through your major identity issues, then try the next step. If, after you've started the next step, you hit a roadblock or something comes up that lets you know you need more time dwelling in the disconnection zone before you move on, then do that. The great thing about this decision is that the next step is not jumping back into the old routine, so it's easy to go back and forth between this step and the next one if you feel the need.

During this disconnecting to re-engage process, you'll experience the healing power of the Gospel and make progress in getting free from the performance trap. That feels great. It should be a time of deepening your relationship with God and a time of increasing peace in your soul as you truly internalize the truth that your value and worth are independent of your performance. But there's another important piece of the foundation that must be laid during this phase of your journey.

In order to properly discern what God's calling for your life is, you need to re-wire your thinking and unlearn what you thought you knew about calling and purpose. In its place, you need to establish a correct understanding of God's biblical plan for calling and purpose.

That's the topic of the next chapter, and it's something very different from what you probably expect.

Chapter 8 – What the Bible REALLY Teaches about Calling and Purpose

One of the reasons many of us have had such a hard time wrestling with the issue of calling and purpose in our own lives is because we've had a warped view of what 'calling' is and how God reveals our calling. I've already discussed some of my former views on this topic, and I'm sure you have your own stories to share along these lines. So, in this chapter, we're going to look at what the Bible teaches regarding this topic with fresh eyes. We'll rectify the misconceptions and deliver a clear understanding of calling and purpose that will enable you to move on to the next step in your journey of discovering and living out your calling.

To start off our re-orientation, I offer up what may be a ground-breaking truth for some of us:

The Bible does not teach that God will tell you what your unique, individual calling is.

Mind blown.

"But that can't possibly be true!" you might be saying. "What about Moses and the burning bush, Samuel anointing David to be King, Gabriel visiting Mary to tell her she would give birth to Christ?" Yes, all of those individuals and many more in the Biblical narrative had their specific life callings revealed to them very clearly. In fact, the Bible is literally replete with examples of individuals who had their specific, individual life's calling delivered to them on a silver platter in a supernatural way. So, how can I possibly be right when I tell you that the Bible doesn't teach that we should all expect the same thing?

Because, quite simply, the Bible never states that this same kind of experience will happen for every believer. Neither does it teach that God will plainly tell *most* believers what their specific, unique calling is. In fact, most people mentioned in the Bible by name don't have their individual life's calling told to them in the Biblical narrative.

So, why do so many people expect that God will tell them what their life's calling is?

For starters, with so many of the prominent Biblical characters having their life's calling told to them in a dramatic fashion, it's easy, as a reader of the Bible, to **assume** that God's plan is to do the same for everyone else, too. Now, we may not expect an angelic visitation or to see a burning bush in our front yard, but it is quite reasonable that we would assume from the Biblical narrative that, at some point in our lives, when we are ready, God will tell us what our life's calling is. But this belief is the result of lazy thinking and poor Biblical scholarship.

As this point began to clarify in my mind, I realized that I had not done the hard work of digging into this topic, but had instead embraced a surface perception as the bed-rock truth—and I was wrong. I had internalized a false belief, and it had warped my understanding of calling and purpose for decades. The truth, however, is much simpler. What the Bible is teaching us through these many stories of dramatically revealed life callings is that God *sometimes,* and *as He chooses,* decides to reveal a person's unique, individual calling to them in a clear manner in a single supernatural encounter. But the Bible never explicitly states that this will be the case for everyone. If it happens with you at some point in your journey, great—but the chances are that it won't.

So, what's the good news?

The good news is that God's Word does teach us that every person has a unique calling, and the Bible does teach us how we can discern our own calling in partnership with the Holy Spirit. Let's take a look at each of these points, in turn.

We each have a unique calling

There are many scriptures and teachings in the Bible that support the belief that each of us has a unique calling. One of the clearest examples is found in the Book of Jeremiah, Chapter 29, Verse 11:

> ***'For I know the plans that I have for you,' declares the LORD, 'plans for welfare and not for***

calamity to give you a future and a hope.'

You can rest assured in the fact that God has a specific plan for your life. King David records an equally powerful truth in the book of Psalms, Chapter 139, Verse 16. In a passage where David is addressing God, he states:

> ***Your eyes have seen my unformed substance; and in Your book were all written the days that were ordained*** FOR ME, ***when as yet there was not one of them.***

These verses, and many others in the Bible, make it very clear that God has a unique plan for each person and that He is interested and concerned enough about that plan to record every detail of each of our individual lives in Heaven. That's amazing. But, if that's true, then how is it that so many of us have a difficult time discovering God's unique, individual plan for our own life?

A revealing parable

This chapter is about re-learning. It is about laying aside one incorrect way of thinking and believing, and choosing as an act of our will and faith to pick up and adopt a new way of thinking and living. Who better to help us along in that process than Jesus Himself?

As I have previously mentioned, it was when I was working through my own season of disconnecting and re-engaging with the Gospel that I re-discovered Jesus' teaching on 'The Parable of the Talents'. Suddenly, I saw the truths being revealed in this parable concerning calling and purpose, as if for the first time. The story is located in a passage where Jesus is teaching a series of parables describing what the kingdom of God is like. It's re-printed below from the New American Standard translation (Matthew 25:14-30):

> *For [it is] just like a man [about] to go on a journey, who called his own slaves and entrusted his possessions to them. To one he gave five talents, to another, two, and to another, one, each according to his own ability; and he went on his journey.*
>
> *Immediately the one who had received the five talents went and traded with them, and gained five more talents. In the same manner the one who [had received] the two [talents] gained two more. But he who received the one [talent] went away, and dug [a*

hole] in the ground and hid his master's money.

Now after a long time the master of those slaves came and settled accounts with them. The one who had received the five talents came up and brought five more talents, saying, "Master, you entrusted five talents to me. See, I have gained five more talents." His master said to him, "Well done, good and faithful slave. You were faithful with a few things, I will put you in charge of many things; enter into the joy of your master."

Also the one who [had received] the two talents came up and said, "Master, you entrusted two talents to me. See, I have gained two more talents." His master said to him, "Well done, good and faithful slave. You were faithful with a few things, I will put you in charge of many things; enter into the joy of your master."

And the one also who had received the one talent came up and said, "Master, I knew you to be a hard man, reaping where you did not sow and gathering where you scattered no [seed.] And I was afraid, and went away and hid your talent in the ground. See, you have what is yours." But his master answered and said to him, "You wicked, lazy slave, you knew that I reap where I did not sow and gather where I scattered no [seed.] Then you ought to have put my money in the bank, and on my arrival I would have received my [money] back with interest.

Therefore take away the talent from him, and give it to the one who has the ten talents."

For to everyone who has, [more] shall be given, and he will have an abundance; but from the one who does not have, even what he does have shall be taken away. Throw out the worthless slave into the outer darkness; in that place there will be weeping and gnashing of teeth.

While the word 'talent' in the story refers to a unit of money, I think you will see by the end of this chapter that it also fits in perfectly with the topic we are discussing to think of 'talent' in this parable as referring to an alternate definition of the term—a gift or ability.

So, what do we learn from this parable?

Let's re-cap the main points of the story. Three servants are entrusted with various amounts of money before their master goes on a long journey. Upon his return, the master calls on all three servants to give an account of what they have done with the funds he entrusted to each of them. The first two doubled the amount of money by investing it somehow—how, exactly, we aren't told. The third servant returns to the master exactly what he was given to begin with, having simply buried it in the ground and not attempted to invest it at all. The master rewards the first two servants for having produced an increase with what he entrusted to them and punishes the third for not having produced an increase.

At first blush, this story could be interpreted by some—very simplistically—to mean that God has given us all resources in varying degrees, and that He expects us to produce a return on His investment or else be punished severely. I would suggest that that interpretation falls far short of what Jesus was teaching us here.

As we look closer at the details of the story, some interesting things begin to come to light. To begin with, it is noteworthy that the master in the story doesn't tell the servants what to do with this money. However, from the way the servants react upon his return, it is obvious that they understood that the master wanted a return on his investment. Another interesting point regarding the parable is that it never mentions what the servants did to generate an increase. We don't know if they bought and sold merchandise, or if they invested in agriculture, or what other enterprise they might have engaged in. We'll come back to these two points momentarily. First, let's take a look at another passage in the New Testament that teaches on a similar topic.

In 1 Corinthians 12:7-11, the Apostle Paul says the following:

> *Now to each one the manifestation of the Spirit is given for the common good. To one there is given through the Spirit a message of wisdom, to another a message of knowledge by means of the same Spirit, to another faith by the same Spirit, to another gifts of healing by that one Spirit, to another miraculous powers, to another prophecy, to another distinguishing between spirits, to another speaking in different kinds of tongues, and to still another the interpretation of tongues.*
>
> *All these are the work of one and the same Spirit, and he*

distributes them to each one, just as he determines.

It is clear from this passage that God doesn't equip everyone with the same gifts, talents, and abilities. It is also clear that everyone receives at least one gift, talent, or ability, and that the purpose of these endowments is to benefit the larger whole of society, or, that they are intended 'for the common good'. This theme is made clear throughout the New Testament—that each believer has a responsibility to build the kingdom of God on Earth by using the unique gifts, talents, and abilities that they have been blessed with. This, in conjunction with our relationship with God, is what gives our lives purpose, meaning, and fulfillment and is at the core of what a calling is.

The kingdom of God can be defined in very basic terms as the rule and reign of Jesus

Christ over all creation. Essentially, to build the kingdom of God on Earth means to bring all good things that God wants us to experience into reality in every possible way, wherever you are. Where there is sickness, bring health. Where there is poverty, bring abundance. Where there is strife, bring peace. I could go on and on here, but describing the totality of what the kingdom of God means is beyond the scope of this book. For a deeper understanding of this topic, I suggest you read the New Testament—specifically, the life of Jesus in the Gospels.

The kingdom of God can also be understood in this way: It means having a right relationship with God through the spiritual re-birth of salvation, thereby gaining access to all of God's limitless resources for doing good, and then using those resources to help others to experience the same transformation and goodness. There are a million different ways this can be expressed, from giving a cup of cold water to someone who is thirsty to developing a cure for a disease in a laboratory. Taking the resources you have and using them to make the world a better place is helping to manifest the kingdom of God in our world.

At this point, we've made a connection between the parable of the talents and the way God wants us to live. Just as the servants in the story were given resources to invest in expanding their master's kingdom, so also each of us has been given at least one gift, talent, or ability that we are to use in expanding God's kingdom here on Earth. The process of doing this is the fulfillment of our calling.

Okay, so far, we probably haven't covered much new ground. If you have been in church for very long, you probably already knew most of what I've covered in this chapter. But here is where we step off into the deep end and begin to unravel the keys that are going to help launch you into the discovery of your own personal calling. It has to do with the two seemingly minor points that I made earlier. Firstly, that the master in the parable never tells the servants what to do with the resources he entrusted them with. Secondly, the parable never says what the two profitable servants did with those resources in order to produce an increase for their master.

More questions to ponder

As I was going through the disconnection process in my own life and re-engaging with the Gospel, two questions came to the forefront of my mind. One of them I've already mentioned. The two questions were, "Will God ever tell me what my calling is?" and, "If God never tells me what my calling is, how will I live?"

We've already discussed that God never promises in the scriptures that He will tell us what our individual callings are. He might tell you today, or He might never tell you. There's no guarantee either way. So, I reasoned, if He might not ever tell me, then I have another question I need to answer. How am I going to live the rest of my life if He doesn't tell me what my calling is?

I had struggled off and on with depression for years, and I had also invested a great deal of time and effort in church ministries and reached the point of being burned out and unconvinced of what my own calling was. At the same time, I also wasn't happy to simply show up at an unfulfilling job for the rest of my life. I still loved my family and was committed to helping provide for them, and I wanted to stay around to be with them, but I knew I needed something more to really stay in the game—to stay alive on the inside.

The need to know and live out my unique calling was crying out from my soul.

In the midst of wrestling with these questions, I came back to the parable of the talents and started to see the story in a new way. As I did, two curiosities stood out to me. Why didn't the master tell the servants what to do with the resources he'd entrusted to them, and why didn't the parable reveal what activities the two faithful servants undertook in order to produce an increase for their master?

Some may reason that these details weren't mentioned because they weren't necessary in order for Jesus to make the point that He was trying to make. Another person may reason that the servants would already know what the master expected them to do with the resources. But I began to see a different possibility for the absence of these two details. What if the reason that the master didn't tell the servants what specific activity to undertake with the resources was that he was leaving that decision up to them?

In the absence of an answer to my question about what my calling was, I decided to try an experiment.

I decided to give myself a calling.

As I moved ahead with this agenda, I began to ask myself an entirely new question. What would I do with my remaining time on Earth if I could choose to do anything?

Previously, whenever I had considered what I would do with my life, other concerns had heavily influenced my thought process. Would what I busied myself doing provide for the needs of my family, financially? Would it fulfill the larger purpose of advancing the kingdom of God in some way? But at this point, I set those other concerns aside and began to listen to my own self with a new perspective. I was finally secure in God's undying and eternal acceptance of me right where I was and as who I was. This enabled me to listen to my own soul and really discern what my own desires and inclinations were without the pressure to perform for anyone else—even God. I could finally really listen to *me*.

I discovered that I didn't immediately have a clear direction. I had buried my own desires for so long, giving preference to other concerns and motivations, that I didn't have a clear idea of what I would do with my life if I was the one who had the sole power to choose. I wasn't yet sure what I really wanted or desired, specifically.

At this point, I was still in my waiting phase. I had not yet begun the process of filling up my schedule with new commitments that would replace the ones I had left behind when I'd started this journey. I was, in effect, giving myself the gift of boredom. And it was in this space that the seed of calling and desire began to grow.

One of the reasons for disconnecting from old commitments is that it gives us this space, this room to experience a lack of busyness—the room to contemplate and be alone with our own thoughts without the clutter of other influences and pursuits. It allows us to meditate and ponder and become aware of things within ourselves and around us that we were too busy or too overwhelmed or too influenced by others to notice before. And in this space, while I was asking myself what I wanted to do (a question that I wasn't quite sure how to answer yet), that I decided to do something fun.

The power of FUN

Never underestimate the power of fun to reveal to you what your real desires and motivations in life are. I decided that while I was waiting to discern what my real calling was, and as I pondered the calling I might give myself in the absence of a clear direction from God, I would do something fun. This decision had an interesting and far-reaching impact on my life.

For years, I had enjoyed storytelling. From my youngest days, my playtime had usually involved some aspect of storytelling. My toy soldiers weren't just nameless fighters—many of mine had names and backstories, and were a part of an ongoing narrative that would be continued from one play session to the next. As I grew older I stopped telling these stories to myself and my playmates. I began to turn this creative energy toward writing song lyrics, and eventually writing many papers and articles on the Christian faith that would be published on my own now-defunct website. Later I would write course material for classes that I taught at church or sermons that I preached.

As I marinated in the disconnection zone and asked myself the question of the day—*what would I decide to do with my life if I alone were giving the marching orders?*—this latent creative force for telling stories began to rise up. Truth be told, I had played around with writing a novel in recent years, but for one reason or another, I had lost interest in the project and put it aside. Now, however, I decided to pick it back up. Writing a novel was something I would put on my bucket list, if I had one, so why not try my hand at it now? At least it would give me something to do while I tried to figure this whole calling thing out.

And so, I began to write.

Within about six months, I had completed the rough draft of a novel that I would eventually self-publish under the title *Utopian Day*. During the months that I was writing this novel, I continued to wrestle with the aforementioned questions… 'How will I live if God never tells me what my calling is?' and 'What calling would I give myself, if given the chance?'

As a person of faith, and as someone who likes to read good fiction, I have frequently been appalled over the years at how many writers feel compelled to include lascivious, overtly sexual content in their writings, and how much foul language litters the literary landscape of our time. I resolved that my novel would contain none of these things. As I wrote, an idea began to percolate in my brain. I had long been convinced that our nation's entertainment content had led us down the primrose path to embrace ever-increasing sexual immorality and other undesirable behavior. The idea that began to form in my mind was that, if unwholesome entertainment could be used to lead people astray, why couldn't wholesome entertainment be used to help lead people back towards God and the ways of truth and purity?

I began weaving these ideas into the narrative of my book. My goal became, rather than to write a book specifically for the Christian market, to write a book for the secular market that would exhibit Christian values. A book that was entertaining, but which would also plant the idea inside someone's brain that God wasn't their enemy, that it wasn't unusual for people to pray when they were in trouble or otherwise, and that some people actually valued sexual morals (and it wasn't a bad thing). By the time I had completed writing the book, I had also developed a very clear vision for utilizing my creative ability in this medium to build God's kingdom. And what's more, I was having FUN doing it.

Now, anyone who tells you that writing and publishing a novel doesn't involve copious amounts of hard work has never done it before. But I realized that it was a fulfilling pursuit for me. By the time I had published the book, I knew that, if I had the option, the 'calling' I would give myself would be writing books and stories.

The answer to the questions from the parable

While I was in the process of writing my novel, I was still wrestling with the remaining questions from the parable of the talents, 'Why didn't the master tell the servants what to do with the resources he entrusted to them?' and 'Why didn't the parable identify what activities the two faithful servants undertook in order to produce an increase for their master?' Once I had completed the novel, I was able to imagine the answers to these questions and put together the pieces of the calling puzzle that had eluded me for so long.

In the process of meditating on the parable, I began asking myself other questions. What if God was telling us, through this little parable, that He wanted *us* to help decide what our calling would be? What if God's method of revealing our calling was to work alongside us, to lead us through our desires and inclinations—

to include us as thinking, creative, emotional beings in the process of discerning our own calling? Perhaps why He didn't say what these two productive servants did with the resources entrusted to them was because He meant to illustrate the idea that the specific task we apply our gifts, talents, and abilities to in life isn't the point. What if, instead, the point is that we actually should get out there and use our gifts, talents, and abilities to produce something for His kingdom—and how we do that is up to us to decide (along with the often unrecognized but very active guiding hand of the Holy Spirit)?

What if?

'What if?' is a big question. It can be an empowering one or a limiting one, depending on how you answer it in a given situation. 'What if God doesn't tell me what my calling is?' can lead to despair and depression, or it can lead you to the point where you actually consider that there might be an answer to the question that sets you free.

For me, these questions and the possible answers that I began entertaining ultimately led to a radically different paradigm than the one I had begun with. Instead of continuing to sit around and wait for God to reveal my calling in some supernatural encounter, in this new way of thinking, I would be an active participant, working alongside God in discovering my calling.

I began to examine the implications of in the light of everything the Bible teaches about calling and purpose to see if there was a contradiction or fallacy in my thought process—some way that this new paradigm violated a Biblical truth—and I found none.

Thinking about the process of finding my calling in this new light felt right. It didn't contradict Biblical teaching, and it answered many of my questions. As the certainty grew in my heart and mind that this interpretation was actually correct, I felt something else begin to stir in my soul—hope.

By taking my questions and turning them into statements, I come up with the following:

God wants *us* to help decide what our calling will be. God's method of revealing our calling is to work alongside us, to lead us through our desires and inclinations—to include us as thinking, creative, emotional beings in the process of discerning our own calling.

After years of wrestling with the questions surrounding calling in my own life, I made a decision that would change everything. I decided to embrace these statements as truth. Once I did, I felt a release that was life-changing.

Because of the path God had led me on, I instantly knew what my calling would be—to write. It would take more time to work through exactly what that would look like. In fact, that's a wonderful part of this ever-changing journey. There continue to be ups and downs, and I continue to grow in my understanding and confidence in God's process. But the knowledge of what my calling is has been settled.

While some might say it happened by accident, I know that God was gently teaching me the principles that I am privileged to help relay to you in this book. He was teaching me the way to discern what my calling was. He didn't TELL me what my calling was—nor did He ever promise to. But God did help REVEAL what my calling was through the process I am teaching in this book.

The difference between telling and revealing is an important distinction. In the writing craft, a frequent and time-honored piece of advice is, 'Show, don't tell.' The reason we do this is that 'showing' is a much more fulfilling experience for the reader; they connect with the emotions of a scene much more concisely and deeply than if they are simply told about what happened. Think of telling a child that the stove is hot and that they shouldn't touch it. Now imagine instead that you carefully guide their hand close enough to the hot eye to let them feel the heat for themselves without getting burned—which, do you think, will create a more lasting and correct impression of the dangers of touching a hot stove? In revealing our calling to us instead of telling us outright, God is using a similar process.

What began as a bucket list project undertaken in the midst of my ponderings on the parable of the talents had been the vehicle that God used to help reveal my calling. And, more importantly, it helped teach me the way others could discern their own calling, too.

During my journey to search for my calling, I went through a full range of emotions and states of thought. At first, I was mad at God, depressed, and even experiencing despair. But as I continued the journey I was on and continued to meditate on the truth of the Gospel, I realized that this God Who had lived a human life and died a horrible death so that He could spend eternity with me wasn't a sadist. He wasn't cruel. He loved me. And if He loved me that much, then God's plan for my life couldn't be some cruel joke or a pointless hardship. There had to be answers to my questions about my calling that were life-giving.

Jesus said, 'Know the truth, and the truth will set you free.' But on the road to freedom, there are often many detours that lead us through some rough neighborhoods. Where you end up depends on who you are following. I had gone through many dark places along my journey to the truth, and finally, the light had dawned.

A third question from the parable

There is one more jewel that I want to mine from the parable of the talents before we move on, and it comes in the form of another question. In the parable, the two servants who invested their resources both gained an increase. But logic, experience, and even a passing knowledge of human history demonstrate that this isn't always the case when people set out to reach a goal. Failure, in the real world, is a very possible outcome of making an investment. So what gives?

Is Jesus painting a pie-in-the-sky picture for us that doesn't bear out in reality? What if we give it our best shot and invest our gifts, talents, and abilities in life only to fail? What if we don't actually accomplish the task of making the world a better place as a result of our efforts? What then?

I believe that God is giving us a great encouragement in this parable—an encouragement that is borne out by other teachings throughout the Bible in both the Old and New Testaments. The reason that the parable doesn't contain a third type of person—one who invested their resources and yet failed to produce an increase—is because, when we invest our gifts, talents, and abilities to make the world a better place (i.e. to build the kingdom of God), we CANNOT FAIL.

Pause and think about that for a minute.

Read this statement again and really let it sink in.

When we invest our gifts, talents, and abilities to make the world a better place we CANNOT FAIL.

'But wait a minute,' some might say, 'you said it yourself—in the real world, people fail all the time.' And that's true. By the standards of human measurement, people fail all the time. But that's in the world's economy. God's economy works differently. In the Bible, in the book of Matthew, Chapter 25, Verses 31-46, Jesus relates a prophecy about what it will be like on the day of judgement, when God evaluates the lives of all humankind:

> ***But when the Son of Man comes in His glory, and all the angels with Him, then He will sit on His glorious throne. All the nations will be gathered before Him; and He will separate them from one another, as the shepherd separates the sheep from the goats; and He will put the sheep on His right, and the goats on the left.***

Then the King will say to those on His right, "Come, you who are blessed of My Father, inherit the kingdom prepared for you from the foundation of the world. For I was hungry, and you gave Me [something] to eat; I was thirsty, and you gave Me [something] to drink; I was a stranger, and you invited Me in; naked, and you clothed Me; I was sick, and you visited Me; I was in prison, and you came to Me."

Then the righteous will answer Him, "Lord, when did we see You hungry, and feed You, or thirsty, and give You [something] to drink? And when did we see You a stranger, and invite You in, or naked, and clothe You? When did we see You sick, or in prison, and come to You?"

The King will answer and say to them, "Truly I say to you, to the extent that you did it to one of these brothers of Mine, [even] the least [of them,] you did it to Me."

Then He will also say to those on His left, "Depart from Me, accursed ones, into the eternal fire which has been prepared for the devil and his angels; for I was hungry, and you gave Me [nothing] to eat; I was thirsty, and you gave Me nothing to drink; I was a stranger, and you did not invite Me in; naked, and you did not clothe Me; sick, and in prison, and you did not visit Me."

Then they themselves also will answer, "Lord, when did we

see You hungry, or thirsty, or a stranger, or naked, or sick, or in prison, and did not take care of You?"

Then He will answer them, "Truly I say to you, to the extent that you did not do it to one of the least of these, you did not do it to Me."

These will go away into eternal punishment, but the righteous into eternal life.

God doesn't evaluate results the way that we do. God measures results on the basis of the heart—whether or not our actions have been motivated out of our love for God and our fellow humans, not on whether or not we wrote a best-selling book, donated millions to charity, or discovered the cure for cancer. The calling that God had in mind for each of us when He made us is rooted in love. You cannot possibly live out your calling the way God intends without love being the prime mover and the chief motivating factor.

At the final judgement, God is looking for those who have invested the gifts, talents, and abilities that He gave them in expressions of love in an effort to help better the lives of others. I don't believe the list mentioned is exhaustive. Feeding the hungry and visiting those in prison can be very real, tangible acts of love that are needed in our world, without question. And so are a hundred-thousand other expressions of love that aren't mentioned here specifically. The point is that loving others is what matters, and this is how the results of your investment are measured by God—the only One Whose opinion matters. And if you use your gifts, talents, and abilities to do that in the process of living out your calling, then you have, by God's definition, produced an increase for the kingdom of God that will be rewarded. This is true regardless of how other human beings may evaluate your efforts.

This is a game-changer.

Meditating on the Gospel during this period of disconnecting from the busy-ness of life has hopefully freed you from the pressure to perform in order to be loved, valued, and accepted by God and other human beings. Now, add to that the freedom the knowledge that the results of you living out your calling are not measured by this world's standards, but rather by a loving God. And this loving God simply asks that, whatever you are doing in the process of living out your calling, you let the motivation of love for Him and your fellow human-beings be the guiding force that helps direct your efforts. When this settles in your soul, when it seeps into your bones and becomes a part of your spiritual DNA, you... will... SOAR.

The freedom that comes from embracing this truth is hard to describe. For me—and I'm still learning to embrace it on a daily basis—it makes the journey so much more enjoyable and fulfilling. Now that I don't feel the need to deliver what the world would consider to be tangible results for my efforts in order to succeed in my calling, but can allow God to produce the results in His way and in His timing instead, I feel as if a HUGE weight has been lifted off of my shoulders.

Remember, as Paul so adequately put it in 1st Corinthians 3:7, "So then neither the one who plants nor the one who waters is anything, but God who causes the growth." God is the One Who blesses the efforts we make in seeking to live out our calling, and it is God who produces the growth. He is the One Who decides what that growth should look like—not us. I encourage you to release any internal requirements you have that the results of your efforts must look a certain way. Let God be in control of the results instead. You will be much happier and fulfilled on your journey if you do. It's okay to have goals, but being rigid and inflexible regarding what success may or may not look like will often result in dissatisfaction, disillusionment, and discouragement. I discuss a better way to set goals as you live out your calling in my book, *Overcome the Obstacles and Succeed at Your Calling.*

Even after I had determined that my calling was to write, I struggled with this concept. I invest time, money, and effort in producing a quality book or short story. Beyond the time and effort required to write a good book, I study marketing and make efforts to sell the books, get reviews, distribute the books to retailers, go to writers' conventions, attend writing critique meetings to improve my work, hire a professional editor, and so on and so forth. I'm not doing all of this because results don't matter to me. I'm doing these things so that my writing can have as far-reaching an effect as possible, and one of the tangible evidences of that is, quite simply, the number of copies sold.

And yet, at the end of the day, I have to realize that not every author becomes a national sensation or a household name. Not every author sells enough books to make a living by their writing or achieve best-seller status. In fact, statistically in the industry, most books on the bookstore shelves actually lose money. Most authors don't make enough money from their craft to write as their primary source of income. With the understanding that over a million books are published annually in the United States, you can begin to understand the challenge it is to stand out and rise above the crowd to succeed in this way. If I am chasing the brass ring of making a good living as an author and becoming a best-selling author by the standards of the publishing industry, there is a better than average chance that I won't achieve that goal, statistically speaking. If I got up every day with the notion that my success in living out my calling was measured by the worldly standards of what it means to be a success in the publishing industry, then I could very easily be consumed by stress, worry, fear, and discouragement. After all, as of this writing, I haven't yet achieved those milestones, and there is no guarantee that I ever will.

Does that mean I should give up or that I haven't been a success in living out my calling?

No way!

If I didn't embrace the truth that I'm talking about in these pages, the above facts I've just mentioned could be depressing, even crippling. But since I DO embrace the truth, I can get up every day and apply my best efforts to the tasks at hand: to write, market, publish, and distribute these books and writings to the best of my ability, and enjoy the process without the stress of feeling that I will be a failure if I don't achieve certain worldly markers of success. To be sure, I would like to achieve those things, but ultimately, God is the One Who is in charge of the results of my efforts.

I choose to focus on what I am in charge of: working hard to use the gifts, talents, and abilities He has entrusted me with to make the world a better place. As long as I focus on my part and let God do His part, I can be happy and fulfilled right where I am. I am working for God's kingdom. The trappings of worldly success are nice when they come, but they are not the standard by which I measure my success in living out my calling. The closer you can come to staying in this mindset, the more enjoyable and fulfilling you will find the journey as you live out your calling.

Another encouraging scripture to ponder as we contemplate this whole idea of how we should measure success at a given task is found in the book of Romans, Chapter 8, Verse 28: "And we know that God causes all things to work together for good to those who love God, to those who are called according to HIS purpose." Think for a moment, if you will, about the life and death of Christ—not the resurrection and what came afterward, but just up to the point where Jesus died on the cross and was buried in a borrowed tomb. From the human perspective, His life had just ended in defeat, not victory. At that point, from a human perspective, He had failed to accomplish the task of establishing the kingdom of God on Earth. Yet, from God's perspective, He had just accomplished the greatest revolutionary act in the history of the world. He had just become the spotless, sinless sacrifice that would enable all of humanity to be forgiven for our many sins and inherit eternal life through Jesus the Christ. It is a great illustration to consider when pondering what appears through human eyes to be either the success or failure of our efforts to live out our unique calling.

It is impossible for us to see the eternal effects of our labors while we are here in this life. What appears as failure to one person can actually be a huge success in God's eyes, and vice versa. But, there is one thing that you can be absolutely certain of. A genuine act of love in the effort to build God's kingdom can never be a failure, even if it is executed imperfectly. I believe this is what it means to say that all things work together for good for those who love God and are *called* according to His purposes. Or, another way to say it is that all things work together for good for those who love God and are living out their *calling* in an effort to bring God's kingdom on Earth and make the world a better place.

One single act of kindness or generosity can be the difference between life and death for someone else. Your gift of baked goods to a stranger can give them hope to live another day as they witness kindness from another human being just when they thought no one cared. Your interaction with a co-worker on the job can help move them one step closer to finding true peace in Christ Jesus. The song or poem you wrote can help bring happiness to someone's day. The cup of water that you give to a thirsty soul.... The list of possibilities is endless.

Summing it up

I hope this chapter has challenged you to re-think how you view calling and purpose. For most of humanity, our personal, unique calling isn't revealed in a vision or an encounter with an angel, nor is it delivered in an email to our inbox or via the post office. For most of us, finding our personal calling is a collaborative process with God that can be confusing and frustrating, especially if we come to the table with our own misconceptions about God, calling, and our own identity. What I've explained in this chapter is that it doesn't have to be either confusing or frustrating. In fact, the process *can* actually be fun once we get our minds right and begin thinking accurately, once we are free from the lies we have believed and embrace the truth.

In the next chapter, we'll build on the concepts discussed in this chapter and describe the next phase in your journey of discerning and living out your calling. We'll discuss the process of putting action to your knowledge as you begin to DREAM.

Chapter 9 - Learning to Dream and Find Your Calling

In the not too distant past of human history, there was a time when no one had ever been recorded as running a four-minute mile. Today, this milestone in running ability—while still impressive—has been achieved by many high-school-aged athletes. Why the change? The change came when a man named Roger Bannister decided that he had the potential to break this record and set out to make it a reality. While it had never been done before, Roger embraced the belief that he *could* run a mile in less than four minutes... and he eventually did it.

But he didn't do it by waking up one day, having the idea pop into his head, and then putting on his running shoes right then and making history. He trained first. And the training was long and hard, and it didn't just include physical training. There was the mental training required for him to learn to believe something was possible that had never been done before.

Just like Roger's dream to break the four-minute mile, finding your calling is a *process*.

In the previous chapters of this book, I've described a process by which you can be transformed into a person who can and will successfully discern and live out your calling. If you've begun to implement the techniques and steps we've discussed so far, it may be that you are reading this chapter at the same time as you are actively planning your temporary disconnection from unnecessary commitments. Or, perhaps you are farther along than this and you have recently arrived at the point where you are now free from such commitments. Hopefully, at whatever point you are on your journey, you are continuing to journal and think on the questions I've posed, and meditating on the Gospel frequently. These techniques will help you to truly stop living in the trap of trying to validate your value and worth by performing for God and humankind. My prayer is that you are now actively choosing to embrace the fact that it is enough for you to simply BE a child of God.

If you are in the process of doing these things, then great. However, I will offer a word of caution here. Unless you have already completed your time of temporarily disconnecting from unnecessary commitments, regardless of how long that may take, then you are likely not yet ready to implement the steps I will lay out in this chapter.

And that's okay.

Read the chapter anyway, but realize that, just like those early athletes who broke the four-minute mile barrier, you first have to train and prepare yourself to reach the state of mind and heart required to discern your calling. Then, once you have completed the previously outlined steps, come back and read this chapter again and implement the steps I will outline below.

The truth is that, unless you are prepared by completing the previous steps, you are likely still heavily influenced by your old thought patterns of what you 'should' be doing with your life, or what other significant people in your life want you to do, or what you erroneously think that God wants you to do with your life. If you are still in that place, then the dreams you come up with at this stage won't be true to what God really has in mind for you, and at the end of this process, you'll be back in the same place you were when you started this book—trying to discern and live out your calling in a way that just doesn't work.

So, that said, let's begin to discuss the dreaming process.

The dreaming process

At this point, it's not yet time to return to old commitments. It isn't time to make new commitments yet, either. But it *is* time to dream. This will be directed dreaming. Don't brainstorm about what you are going to do to help make the world a better place; don't even try to discern what it is you are called to do with your life at this point. Instead, what I want you to dream about is what you would like to do for FUN.

God has designed us as emotional beings. Science has helped us learn a great deal about God's design. For instance, we know that we need sleep not only to rest our physical bodies, but so that we can dream (Carr, 2017). We tap into a similarly powerful dynamic when we dream while we are awake. Dreaming helps us tap into the ability to see beyond where we are and peer into the realm of what might be. When we dream, we are exercising our ability to envision something that exists only in the realm of possibility.

So, in an act of faith, I want you to begin asking some questions of yourself. Remember, the goal here is to dream about things you would like to do that are FUN—things you would actually enjoy doing. If you could do anything for the rest of your life without concerning yourself with what your calling in life is, what would it be? What are some things on your bucket list that you've always wanted to do? What is some activity—old or new—that you would like to do again or try for the first time?

Have you always dreamed of hiking across Europe or on the Appalachian Trail? Have you always wanted to learn how to fly? What about writing a novel? Do you love to bake so much that you can see yourself baking things for others even when you retire? Does helping out at the homeless shelter really make you feel fulfilled? Do you enjoy organizing social events or public speaking? Do you enjoy gardening and long for each new growing season to begin?

This isn't the time to think about others first. It is the time to think about what makes YOU happy. What do YOU enjoy doing?

By the end of the disconnect and re-engaging season of your journey, you'll hopefully have been freed from those pesky voices in your head and heart concerning what you 'should' be doing, and you can actually drill down to what you - as a unique, creative being - would find enjoyable.

For some people, this will be easy. Maybe you've always enjoyed playing music, and that is a passion that has never wavered throughout your life. Maybe painting is your thing. Or maybe you simply enjoy helping others in practical ways. For others, you may be drawing a blank at this point. You may have no clue what you would actually like to do simply for fun. If you find yourself in this place, then it is time to try something new.

Take a knitting class. Learn to kayak. Read a book on building birdhouses or find a new skill or activity you would like to participate in. One way to get some ideas would be to explore internet sites that promote social activity groups, like Meetup.com (I'm not endorsing all the groups on this site, but there are some good groups to be found there at the time of this writing). Take a dance class. Learn to cook or grow a garden. Start going to the gym or take a Pilates class. Go for a bike ride. The list of possibilities is endless. I encourage you to pray and ask God to help guide you during this process. He is, after all, interested in your life and in your desires and happiness.

The point is that it is time to engage in some activities that you consider fun during the dreaming phase. Don't make a six-month commitment to show up every week at a knitting class if you have no idea whether or not you will like it, or commit to spending the summer feeding the homeless in the downtown district of your city if you have never worked with the homeless before. The point here is to try some things out, not to jump back into long-term commitments. You may discover you really like what you try, or you may discover you hate it. But the experiences will help you begin to get a feel for your own likes and dislikes, freed from the influences of others and the felt need to perform in order to confirm your own value and worth in the universe.

As you go through this phase, do some journaling on why you do or do not enjoy the activities you try. Did you find that you didn't really like serving in the food line at the homeless shelter, but you did enjoy talking to the different people and learning about their life stories? Were you surprised that you enjoyed a baking class? Was it the being around others engaged in a common task that you enjoyed, or the actual baking process, or both? Spend some time getting to know what you do and don't like and why, and record these thoughts using your journaling process where you can easily look back on it.

As you are moving through this process, keep your eyes open. Remember that you aren't going through this alone. While it may seem that you are the one making all of the decisions, know that God is involved in the process and is guiding your steps (Psalm 37:23).

Finally finding your calling

For many of us, finding our calling is not an epiphany; the calling isn't delivered via a vision or an angelic visitation, but is rather a decision that we make in partnership with God about how we'll choose to invest the resources we have been given by God (i.e. our time, gifts, talents, and abilities). When this decision is made in a guilt-free environment by a person who is practicing BEING, and whose motivation is not selfish ambition, it is much more likely to reflect God's purpose for a person in that moment.

After you purge yourself of the felt need to generate your personal significance or worth through what you do, you become truly free. In this state of being, the gratitude we have for the great gift of salvation given to us by God combined with our God-given creative passion stirs us to use our gifts, talents, and abilities to make the world a better place, both physically and spiritually. What can start as a simple desire to plant a garden for our own enjoyment can become a vehicle for blessing others with that same garden's produce – one small expression of God's kingdom come on Earth.

As a believer in Christ Jesus, your true calling will always have a connection with the Gospel. As I've mentioned before, this can manifest in a million different ways. But as you go through this process of getting in touch with your true likes and dislikes as a unique individual, at some point, the Holy Spirit (God's guiding light within you) is going to spark a thought in your brain. At some point, you are going to see an opportunity to do something to meet a need that someone else has. In this process of engaging in divinely inspired play and fun, a thought will begin to form in your mind. And you are going to experience—perhaps for the first time in your life—the genuine, Holy Spirit inspired nudge of God's calling.

Now, you and I both see needs that others have every day. There are many things we can do to help others, and we could all make a list right now of probably ten things that we could do tomorrow to help someone else. The difference here is that, when you see this particular need, you will begin to get a vision for helping to meet this need in a way that is connected to a task or activity that you have already discovered that you enjoy. This will be a need connected to your unique calling. It will be a need that will require that you use your unique gifts, talents, and abilities in order to meet it. And the possibilities will EXCITE you.

When that happens, that's when you really begin to dream. When that happens, let your imagination run wild. Imagine the possibilities. Don't let the practical side of your brain shut it down. DREAM. Imagine what it COULD be like. Don't focus on the obstacles. Focus on what you would like to see happen. If you could write a script for how the situation would unfold and how you would use your gifts, abilities, and talents to meet the need, how would you like the script to play out?

How to transition from dreaming and 'fun' into meeting a need:

Let's look at an example of how the power of dreaming and having fun can be utilized to help you discern your calling.

Suppose the passion you discover while beginning to dream is running. You've gotten to the point that it's obvious that running isn't a short-term obsession, but rather a long-term passion that you want to participate in for as long as you can. Great. How do you possibly make the jump from this point to something akin to a calling?

Remember that you aren't in this alone. God is helping to guide you through the process. If you ask God to help show you an opportunity to use your passion for running in a way that will help others, He will.

So, you pray for God's guidance, and you continue hanging out in the disconnection zone.

One day, while you're running at the local park, you see a group of runners comprised of young adults as well as people your age. A thought sparks in your brain. You've worked with the youth group in the past and found that you liked interacting with the kids, but just didn't seem to connect with their interests enough to help mentor them effectively. What if you could connect with young people through a running group and possibly develop mentoring relationships with them in that context? Bingo, you've just come up with a way to help meet a need utilizing your unique gifts, talents, abilities, and desires.

Hang out in the dreaming phase for a while. Similar to the disconnection and re-engagement phase, it is important that you don't rush this process. It may take you many months or more than a year to discover that 'aha!' moment when you finally find something that excites you, which you think you could participate in for the long-term, and which you can envision doing in a way that helps meet a need in the lives of others. Once you have discovered what that is, then it is time to move on to the final phase of the process.

How to name your calling

You have found your calling when you are passionately using your gifts, talents, and abilities to make the world a better place—either physically, spiritually, or both. Far from being some mystical process shrouded in secrecy, your calling is something that God wants to lead you to discover alongside Him as you experience life and develop the gifts, talents, and abilities that He has placed within you.

So, how do you take this last step? How do you take all of the lessons you've learned about God, yourself, and this thing we call 'calling', and make the final decision about what your calling is? Yes, that's right, how do YOU make that final decision about what your calling is and give it substance?

God has been guiding you all along. If you have followed the process I've described in this book, you aren't just making a stab in the dark; you've been following a path that has helped equip you to make this decision. You haven't been rushing things. Now, it is time to have faith in God and in the process, and make a divinely influenced decision.

Much like the disconnection and re-engaging phase, the dreaming phase can't be held to a specific timetable. For me, it was about a six-month process. By the time I had finished writing my first novel, I knew it was something I wanted to do for the rest of my life and I had a vision for using this gift to bless others. For some of you, the realization of what you are passionate about doing and how you can do it to bless others will come more quickly, and for others it may take a bit longer.

The truth is that YOU are empowered to decide what your calling is as you walk in relationship with God and follow the guideposts of your own desires, gifts, talents, abilities, and opportunities. God has designed the process to work in this way. Embrace this responsibility as the tremendous gift that it is.

I want you to take some time when you arrive at this point in the process and WRITE DOWN your calling statement. It doesn't have to be ten pages long or even a full paragraph. Here are some examples:

- I am called to use my love for baking to show God's love to others in a tangible way. One way I will do this is by giving these baked goods to people in shut-ins.

- I am called to mentor others on my job so that they can be better at <u>[fill in the blank here with your profession]   </u>. In my mentoring relationships, I will pray for opportunities to let the light of Christ shine through me and help influence others with the message of Christ Jesus.
- I am called to be a painter. I will sell my paintings and help support worthy causes that help improve people's lives, including missionary organizations, with a portion of the proceeds.
- I am called to pray for the needs of others. I will utilize this gift as part of the church prayer team and by praying for those around me on a regular basis.

Over time, continue to refine this description of your calling. You could even call it your personal mission statement. I eventually published a version of my own calling statement on my website, which you can read in the 'about' section of my website https://fictionwithamission.com.

What if you can't decide?

You might possibly come to this point in your journey without having one specific idea about what your calling should be. Or, it might be possible you still haven't thought of *any* possibilities that excite you. If you find yourself in either of these positions, don't despair. In either of these cases, you have been empowered by your Creator to DECIDE.

In the case of having a number of options you are considering, pick one and focus on that for a while, and then re-evaluate your options.

If, on the other hand, you haven't yet hit on an opportunity that excites you, then you may need to continue in the dreaming phase or possibly do some research to find out how others around the world are using a passion similar to yours to help people. Internet search engines can be a great help here. For instance, if you are really into gaming, try a search using the terms, 'gaming helping others'. When I did this, one of the first links returned was entitled, 'Helping others during Covid-19 through gaming'. This tactic should help spark an idea of something you could try.

Whatever you decide to do, it is important to step out in faith and begin moving forward. You won't help anyone if all you do is plan. In time, as you continue to observe and listen to your own thoughts and feelings, and watch for God to reveal opportunities around you, you will continue to refine your understanding and choice of your calling.

Whoever you are, and whatever your abilities may be, there is something you can do to help make the world a better place—both physically and spiritually. Now is the time to take your gifts, talents, and resources, and decide to do something to make that happen. Who knows but that God is waiting on you to take this step of faith before He guides you to the experience that will clarify exactly what will bring you fulfillment through your service? Perhaps, for you, He wants you to serve Him in faith first, before you discover the idea of what will become your life's calling.

Pursuing your calling

Once you have identified your own personal calling, it will likely feel like a huge weight has been lifted off of your shoulders. Now that you understand the cooperative nature of the process involving God and yourself, and you are free from the self-destructive human-pleasing and selfishly ambitious motivations of the past, you can finally begin pursuing what you are called to do without those negative motivations weighing you down. Congratulations! This is truly a time to celebrate!

This is the beginning of a wonderful part of your journey as a believer. In book two of the *Find Your Calling* series, *Overcome the Obstacles and Succeed at Your Calling,* we'll take a look at some of the obstacles and challenges of living out your calling in a fallen world, and help prepare you to successfully live out your calling in the long term.

Bibliography

Carr, Michelle (2017). Dream Deprived: A Modern Epidemic. Psychology Today. Retrieved February 7, 2020 from https://www.psychologytoday.com/us/blog/dream-factory/201708/dream-deprived-modern-epidemic

Hamilton, B., Bundschuh, R., Berk, S. (2006). Soul Surfer: A True Story of Faith, Family, and Fighting to Get Back on the Board. New York, NY: Gallery Books.

Overcome the Obstacles and Succeed at Your Calling

(Book 2 in the Find Your Calling Series)

by

Christopher Wells

www.fictionwithamission.com

clwells@fictionwithamission.com

Chapter 1 – How Do You Define Success?

In book 1 of the Find Your Calling series (entitled *Find Your Calling Without Losing Your Mind)* I detailed a process by which a person could find their life's true calling. If you already know what your calling in life is because you've worked through the material in that book, or if you've come to discover your calling through some other means, I congratulate you. I celebrate with you. I jump up and down and shout, "Yes!" with you. We fist-bump and high-five each other, as this is a truly momentous occasion that should be celebrated and enjoyed for the significant milestone that it is. And after the celebration is over, you get down to walking out this newly discovered truth, living the life, fulfilling your calling.

Life is good.

As time moves on, sooner or later, you will come to a place where the excitement and euphoria of finally knowing your calling with certainty will settle down into the new normal. You'll be moving forward, making progress, enjoying the journey—and then you'll hit a rough patch. Maybe your dream of serving on the city council is temporarily quashed when you lose the election, or you have that difficult student who is making going into the classroom to teach every day a Herculean feat of bravery. Perhaps your last three recipes for three-layered cake have all turned out to be duds.

Whatever the specific circumstances, you will find yourself facing a new challenge that seems to you to be very significant. And it is. This is your new Goliath, and he has 'dream-killer' written across the front of his t-shirt. And this Goliath confronts you with a question that you need to answer.

How do I overcome the obstacles in my path and succeed at my calling?

I've done you the favor of cutting to the chase so we can get down to the crux of the matter. The truth is that most of us don't initially realize that discovering our calling is just phase one. It's just like being the champion boxer in the ring in the tenth round of what was supposed to be an easy title defense fight, and beginning to realize that you might lose the title. So, too, it is usually after some time spent wrestling with the challenges that eventually come with living out our calling that we finally realize we're not sure we have what it takes to succeed at living it out to the fullest. There can come a time when what we've envisioned as success seems a million miles away, or to only exist in an alternate universe.

And, in that place, we can begin to waver. We can start to doubt.

For me, in my journey as a writer, this realization took a few years. From 2015, when I published my first book, to around the end of 2018, I was more or less on a roller coaster of success. Okay, it was more like a kiddie roller-coaster where the highs were just blips on the radar, but to me, it was exciting. Early on, it was a thrill to achieve some small encouragement by seeing my book reach into the top-ten of the free title list on Amazon, or to receive a full-read of my manuscript by a small publisher at a book conference.

I was undaunted—for a while. But as I began to learn more and more about the publishing industry, with no publishing contract and abysmal book sales, my initial enthusiasm began to wane. I learned that 1.68 million books were self-published in 2018 (Milliot, 2019), and that most books on the shelves in the brick-and-mortar book stores actually lose money. I found out that it takes about ten years of writing and trying to get your work noticed before the average successful author lands a book contract—and that many authors never reach this milestone.

I could go on, but the point is that I began to get discouraged. I began to wonder if I was going to succeed at this writing thing. The feelings that I had at that point were strangely familiar. They were very similar to the feelings of confusion, hopelessness, and discouragement that I'd felt when I was struggling to find out what my calling was in the first place.

And when I reached that point, I began to have doubts about whether or not this was going to work. I began to feel that I might not succeed at my calling. And I know I'm not alone in that experience. I know that many people—maybe *most* people who ever pursue their true calling—come to a place and time where they feel the same way.

And that's when many people give up on their calling.

In that tough place where the obstacles to success loom large, and you aren't sure you have what it takes to overcome them, that many dreams can and do die. Many people throw in the towel and decide to take the easy way out, only to discover that they are sacrificing their passion for living along with their calling. I'm convinced that many people suffering from depression can trace the root of it to this place.

But that doesn't have to be you.

You *can* beat the odds.

You *can* overcome the obstacles and succeed at your calling.

And I can teach you how to do it.

If you are going to overcome the obstacles and succeed at your calling, you will need to make your way through this valley of the shadow of the death of your calling. In order to do so, you need to learn more about yourself, what drives you, and what real success looks like.

When I came to this place of crisis in my journey, I began thinking of my younger days, when I'd thought I knew what my calling was. I was just waiting for that burning bush moment or undeniable success to confirm that my calling was genuine and to validate my self-worth in the eyes of God and humankind. I was waiting to attain an incredible achievement or experience, an encounter with God that would settle the matter and make all of the waiting and hard work and struggle worth it. But that day never came.

I had certainly experienced some joy and success in the various endeavors I'd pursued. There'd been fruitful ministry, I had helped people, and I'd been using my gifts and abilities, but the solid confirmation I'd been looking for had never come. I had become discouraged, disillusioned, and depressed—the same feelings

I was beginning to feel again in the face of this new challenge.

I knew that something had to change.

I began journaling and praying and analyzing my thought process. And then I realized something. I realized I had a brass ring mentality. Success for me, at that point in my life, could only be experienced when I had that brass ring in my hand. In my mind, I had to achieve a specific level of performance or attain a particular goal before I would consider myself a success.

The problem with this mentality is that the brass ring moments are few and far between in life. We spend the majority of our lives in pursuit of some goal or another. More sales, reaching 'x' number of people, graduating a certain percentage of students, et cetera. And some goals are never attained. Not every football player gets to play for the NFL. Not every good product is profitable in the marketplace. Not every Bible study group stays going long-term. Does that mean that the people pursuing these goals are failures if they don't achieve what they are seeking? No, it doesn't (we'll dig into answering why that's true later). But that was my mentality at the time. I realized this belief was stealing the joy from pursuing my true calling and leading me to a place of discouragement, disillusionment, and borderline depression.

Once again, I found myself battling these old foes. But I was determined to defeat them this time, once and for all, with God's help.

As I began the quest to slay this new dragon that stood between me and successfully living out my calling, I started to clarify my own definition of success. It was a very revealing exercise. It didn't take long for me to discover that my definition of success was firmly rooted and grounded in a secular worldview. In fact, my definition of success was almost indistinguishable from that of any non-Christian writer. I wanted my books to help people, to be widely read, to rise to the top of the popular best-seller lists, and to make enough money through my writing to be able to quit my day job and write full-time. I had defined success by the attainment of certain physically quantifiable accomplishments, and when those goals remained elusive, I began to be discouraged.

If you fight the Devil on his terms, you'll lose every time. If you try to define what it looks like to successfully live out your calling by using a secular worldview of success, you will miss the mark. I'm not saying you won't achieve the same markers of success that the world covets in your efforts to live out your calling. What I'm saying is that, if attaining those markers of success is your focus, you'll very likely sacrifice some important elements of your calling along the way.

For a while, I doubled-down. I took courses on marketing, tried new advertising strategies, and studied the techniques of the successful authors I was seeking to emulate. I learned a great deal. I learned what it would take to be successful at attaining the definition of success that I had in my mind. And… I didn't feel any better. I estimated that, to accomplish what I was trying to accomplish, I would need to spend about ten hours a week on marketing activities. That would be in addition to my writing, family life (married with an eleven-year-old and two adult children), church activities, and, oh, a full-time job. To add to the challenge was the fact that my wife was just beginning a college degree program that would require me to add some additional responsibilities to my plate so that she could pursue her dream of becoming an engineer.

As I considered whether or not to commit to this additional investment of time in my writing pursuits, I realized it just didn't feel right. The timing was off. Now wasn't the time to add another ten hours per week to my already busy schedule. I decided I either had time to write, or time to market my work at a level that could lead to the definition of success I had in mind, but not both. I had a dilemma and didn't know what to do about it.

As I considered my options, I realized that, even if I did commit to spending the extra ten hours per week on marketing activities (or found another way to accomplish those same tasks), I would essentially still be chasing the same brass ring. I would still be defining success in the same way that had previously contributed to my lack of fulfillment and discouragement in pursuing my calling. I was still operating from the mindset that I needed to accomplish 'X' in order to feel validated or successful.

Changing your definition of success

At this point in my journey, I realized I was stuck in a cycle. Even though my understanding of my identity had changed, in practice, I was still living the same way as before – pursuing accomplishment in order to validate my self-worth and prove I was a success at living out my calling.

It occurred to me that I needed to change my definition of success.

At this point, I took a step back and looked at the big picture. What was the purpose of pursuing my calling, anyway? It was to use my God-given gifts, talents, and abilities to make the world a better place, to build the kingdom of God. If that was true, then it wasn't up to me to define what success at doing that looked like. It was up to God.

I had been studying the scriptures for some time, regarding what the Bible teaches us about calling and purpose. I now began the task of learning how God defines success in those endeavors.

For most of us, the act of pursuing our calling will lead us through some difficult times. There will likely be times when you don't look or feel very successful in the way the world defines success. How can you outlast those seasons, persevering to successfully live out your calling, and enjoy the journey at the same time? I believe one of the keys to doing this is learning to adopt the same belief and attitude about success that your Father in Heaven has.

Now, let's turn the page and find out how to do just that.

Chapter 2 - Re-defining Success

How does God define success?

After Jesus tells the parable of the talents in Matthew Chapter 25, He goes on to describe what it will be like on the judgment day, when God decides the fate of every person who has ever lived. It is in that moment that God will decide if each of us has succeeded in life or not. It is the single-greatest reckoning in all of human history. Contained in this passage is a huge spotlight that shines the light of truth on what God considers success, and it has some surprising implications.

> ***But when the Son of Man comes in His glory, and all the angels with Him, then He will sit on His glorious throne. All the nations will be gathered before***

Him; and He will separate them from one another, as the shepherd separates the sheep from the goats; and He will put the sheep on His right, and the goats on the left.

Then the King will say to those on His right, "Come, you who are blessed of My Father, inherit the kingdom prepared for you from the foundation of the world. For I was hungry, and you gave Me [something] to eat; I was thirsty, and you gave Me [something] to drink; I was a stranger, and you invited Me in; naked, and you clothed Me; I was sick, and you visited Me; I was in prison, and you came to Me."

Then the righteous will answer Him, "Lord, when did we see You hungry, and feed You, or thirsty, and give You [something] to drink? And when did we see You a stranger, and invite You in, or naked, and clothe You? When did we see You sick, or in prison, and come to You?"

The King will answer and say to them, "Truly I say to you, to the extent that you did it to one of these brothers of Mine, [even] the least [of them,] you did it to Me." **(Matthew 25:31-40 NASB)**

Feeding the hungry, giving a drink to the thirsty, showing kindness to the stranger, clothing the naked, and visiting the sick and the imprisoned. These are likely not the things you would typically think about when you consider what successfully living out your calling looks like.

Does this mean the whole idea of a unique calling is nonsense? Should we all stop trying to use our unique talents and join the prison ministry at church or the homeless ministry downtown? What does this mean?

There is no doubt that God expects everyone who calls Him Lord and Savior to participate regularly in helping to fulfill these clearly defined needs in a tangible way. To call yourself a believer in Christ and yet fail to help your fellow humans with basic physical and spiritual needs as Jesus describes above is the height of hypocrisy. And, yes, there is more to this passage than first meets the eye concerning what it has to teach us about success in God's eyes.

So, what does this passage teach us?

Success, in God's eyes, doesn't require us to become CEO of a company, cure cancer, or single-handedly stop sex-trafficking in North America. The acts mentioned above are within reach of almost everyone. And, no, I don't think God is saying you are going to Hell if you don't visit someone in prison during your lifetime. The point here is that demonstrating the love of God to our fellow human beings in a practical way is not hard. It simply requires the willingness to love and share what we have with others. And that is what pleases God.

The servants in the parable of the talents were given resources. They were expected to use those resources to accomplish the will of their master. The only one who failed in God's eyes was the one who did not make any attempt to do that. What if God's definition of you succeeding at the calling which He put in your heart and mind is that you simply use those gifts, talents, and abilities in an effort to show love to others? What if simply participating in that effort IS success? What if the act of participating in that effort, and not the results that may or may not come from it, is how God defines success? Not the attainment of any other measurable goal, not the plaque from your church, not the accolades of your fellow humans, not the gratitude of those whom you serve, and—perhaps most importantly in our case—not the worldly accolades and accomplishment that we usually associate with worldly success.

Boom.

Mind blown.

As I began to contemplate this possibility and compare it with my own outlook regarding what success was, I realized that I had fallen into a trap. I realized I'd been chasing something I already had. According to this radically different definition of success, I was already a success. I was using my gifts, talents, and abilities to make the world a better place—to love others in the unique way that God had created me to do so. Yet, I didn't feel that I had achieved that goal. I was still refusing to believe I was successful at my calling until I held that brass ring in my hand, until I had attained that worldly definition of success that I had crafted in my mind.

There are many factors in achieving what you consider worldly success or reaching the sought-after level of accomplishment at your chosen endeavor. From a purely quantitative viewpoint, if there is any degree of difficulty in achieving worldly success as you have defined it, then the possibility exists that you might not achieve it.

The man who invented the computer operating system that was the foundation of Microsoft Windows sold it to Bill Gates for $50,000. Bill Gates built on that man's creation and is now one of the richest men in the world. Comparing the two, who do you believe was more successful? Next, consider a single mom who takes on two jobs and does her best to keep her daughter safe in the crime-ridden neighborhood where they live, all while trying to teach her how to live life God's way. Compare that woman with the woman who becomes the president of a college and leads an institution to educate thousands. Who is more successful?

Worldly success is, at its core, about judging physically measurable accomplishments against a chosen standard. The man who first ran the four-minute mile was considered a huge success in his day. Today, high-school-aged athletes regularly attain that accomplishment. Yesterday's plateau becomes today's starting point. Worldly definitions of success are constantly changing, depending on prevailing public opinion, past accomplishments of others, et cetera. If you are depending on the world's definition of success to tell you that you are a success in fulfilling your calling, then you will be in for a long journey on an unstable road to a destination where you may never arrive.

But there is a better way. There is God's way. And it will liberate you.

As I embraced this new definition of success, the frustration, discouragement, and depressive feelings I had been experiencing began to dissipate. The energy, excitement, and passion for fulfilling my calling began to re-emerge. From a quantitative standpoint, nothing had changed. I still faced the same obstacles that I'd had moments before, regarding the challenge to market my work and gain readers, but the pressure was off. I felt a deeper level of peace—in much the same way I had when I'd first learned how to define my own calling.

From now on, I would seek to live by this new God-defined definition of success. In this new paradigm, success wasn't the carrot at the end of the stick that I could never seem to reach. I no longer had to wait to see if success would be mine after years of sustained effort and cooperating circumstances which were beyond my control. In this new paradigm, I was a success every day that I chose to use my gifts, talents, and abilities in an attempt to make the world a better place—regardless of whether those efforts produced a particular result or not. That shift in thinking was a game-changer. Let me say that again.

> *I am a success every day that I choose to use my gifts, talents, and abilities in an attempt to make the world a better place – regardless of whether those efforts produced a particular result or not.*

Now, I want you to read that again, but this time, read it as a declaration for yourself. I encourage you to read it out loud, as well, as a proclamation of your own belief.

If you use your gifts and abilities to make the world a better place, as you walk in communion with a loving God Who directs your steps, then YOU CANNOT FAIL.

In this new paradigm, the act of pursuing a specific goal pertinent to my calling changes. The over-arching target is no longer achieving the short-term accomplishment itself. It's much larger than that. Whether or not I achieve the immediate thing I am pursuing doesn't determine success or failure in my calling or in my life. Pursuing that goal-of-the day and utilizing my gifts, talents, and abilities to make the world a better place in the process IS success.

This mindset then becomes the answer to the question of how to overcome the obstacles and succeed at your calling. You can transition from thinking that specific temporal markers define your success to living from a different mentality, one where the goal you are currently pursuing becomes simply that—another goal.

Achieving that temporal goal in front of you no longer constitutes success or failure at your calling. It's the way you pursue it that matters. In this new paradigm, success is simply the act of pursuing your calling—wherever you are at right now with whatever level of skill or opportunity you have right now.

For the person who is called to be a healer but who is not yet a doctor, succeeding at your calling may be studying for that next biology exam. For the engineer who feels called to build things, it may simply be showing up the next day at work and using your gifts, talents, and abilities to design the best widget you can. Sure, owning your own company may be a goal that's very important to you, but success for today is using your gifts, talents, and abilities TODAY. And you can do that. For an author—such as myself—a typical goal would be to sell more books and have my writing appreciated by a larger audience. This goal now ceases to define or limit my success. For me, writing this next sentence is success.

Success, then, ceases to be the elusive pot of gold at the end of the rainbow that we may never attain. It ceases to be defined by the not-yet-but-maybe-someday achievement that prevents us from being content or fulfilled in the present. Instead, success is entirely within my grasp TODAY. All that is required is that I decide to pursue my calling today. Choosing to do that and following through—with my imperfect efforts to do so—is success. That mindset makes all the difference.

How do we walk out this new belief?

Replacing an old belief with a new belief is a process. It requires forming new neural pathways in your brain, and it usually doesn't happen overnight. When you face a fresh disappointment, a new challenge to something you wanted to accomplish, your first thought may not be to process the situation in light of this new definition of success that you've chosen to embrace. Your first thought may be to look at it the same way you used to, and then discouragement rears its ugly head. You may feel like you're a failure, or that you couldn't possibly succeed in the face of this new challenge, and that you might as well give up on pursuing your calling and go sit on the beach all day instead.

But that's not who you are. You now know that failure at a particular task or your inability to achieve a particular goal does not define your success or failure at your calling. Don't beat yourself up because your first thought wasn't true to your new belief. Instead, learn how to progressively move to a place where the truth—your new paradigm of success—becomes more and more ingrained in your psyche to the point where, eventually, it will be your most consistent and persistent response to the challenges you face.

In the next chapter, we'll discuss strategies for doing just that, as well as how pursuing specific, measurable goals fits into this new paradigm of success.

Chapter 3 - Renewing Your Mind for Success

Training your mind to operate according to a new definition of success is a critical part of overcoming obstacles so you can succeed at your calling. This chapter will help equip you with some tools to aid you in the process.

Renewing your mind

It's possible to understand the truth about God's definition of success while, at the same time, frequently falling back into thinking according to our old failure-prone discouragement-producing paradigm of success. But by applying certain principles, we can move beyond this experience to a place where the relapses are fewer and farther between, and where the old mindset no longer controls our decision-making process. The Bible describes this process as our being transformed by the renewing of our minds (Romans 12:2). But how do we do that, practically?

Have you ever learned anything the wrong way and then had to re-learn it? It's harder than learning something the right way the first time. Not only do you have to learn to do it the RIGHT way, but you must also un-learn doing it the WRONG way.

For example, I've struggled with being defensive. Years ago, I was horribly defensive whenever I felt I was being accused of doing something wrong. I eventually came to a place where I realized I needed to change so that my defensiveness wouldn't destroy my relationship with those whom I loved. This change didn't happen overnight. There are still times when I am defensive. In the early days of seeking to change, I almost always had that knee-jerk defense reaction even though I had learned techniques for how to listen rather than attack. I would often find myself needing to come back to someone—usually, my wife—and have a do-over conversation. This time, I would consciously force myself to be patient, to avoid lashing out, to accept personal responsibility for my actions, and to empathize with the other person.

Over time, slowly, I began to have more success at not being defensive nearly as often. My relationships improved. I was being transformed.

I have experienced a similar process when changing any long-held belief or mindset in life. It takes time. The good news is that I'm going to share with you some strategies to help you move through the process faster.

Strategy #1: Saturate Your Mind with the Truth

When seeking to replace an old belief with a new one, it is beneficial to saturate your mind with the new belief and to practice talking yourself out of the old one. In the process of changing my mind to embrace this new perspective on success, I had frequent challenges and was often tempted to fall back into the old mindset. When these challenges arose, I found it extremely helpful to meditate on the material I am now presenting in this book. When you face similar challenges, I suggest you pick up this book and re-read some material that is relevant to what you are struggling with. Find a few short passages that are especially meaningful to you, or write something out in your own words, and when the old way of thinking comes to the forefront of your mind, go and read over it. I believe you will find that it helps stop the old thoughts in their tracks and sets you on the right path once again.

In the beginning, you may find it helpful to print out some short passages on index cards and put them in places that you see frequently—

perhaps on the mirror in the bathroom, for instance. The definition of success is a good one to put on an index card, for starters. I suggest that you read it at least once a day until it becomes the default definition of success in your subconscious mind. It will take time. That's okay. Rome wasn't built in a day.

Strategy #2: Think About Your Thought Process

Our core beliefs matter, and we don't always realize when our heart is living differently than our head. Our behavior (i.e., the actions we take) and our emotional state, over time, will demonstrate the truth we really believe, even when the logical part of our mind is convinced that we believe something else entirely. These deeply held beliefs of the past don't always announce themselves on a billboard or a pop-up window on our smartphone whenever they show up to lead us back into the old way of thinking and behaving. Any time we realize that discouragement, disillusionment, and un-fulfillment are beginning to creep back into our lives, it should be a big, red flag that lets us know we have fallen back under the influence of our old beliefs.

Suppose you have a goal that you've been trying to achieve. We'll call this 'goal X'. You've embraced this new way of looking at success as it relates to your calling, and you've been moving forward, but goal X is just not coming to pass the way you planned. Maybe goal X is getting that next promotion at work so that you can have a more significant influence on the direction the company is taking. It could be learning how to conquer the latest equation in a college course so you can complete your degree. Perhaps helping your son finish toilet training is your goal. Whatever goal X is, it has something to do with your calling, and it seems like you are hitting a brick wall in trying to reach it.

You are frustrated. You feel discouraged, and maybe even a little depressed. *DING, DING, DING!* Warning bells should be going off in your head. The source of these negative feelings could be your old mindset about success and calling rearing its ugly head.

The next part is critical. You need to take a step back from the situation and analyze your thoughts in order to determine what specific beliefs are at the source of these negative feelings.

Let's work through an example.

Ted is trying for a promotion at work so that he can utilize his skills in his calling to be a business leader. Ted works hard, applies for the position, and he thinks he's nailed the interview, only to find that his co-worker Jerry got the promotion instead. At first, Ted tries to shake it off. *I'll get the next promotion,* he tells himself.

But as the weeks go by, the disappointment over losing out on this opportunity doesn't subside. Ted continues to feel frustrated, angry, and disappointed. He doesn't feel the same zeal to get up every morning and use his gifts to fulfill his calling the way he previously did. But he's read this book, and he reminds himself that he needs to take this opportunity to analyze his thoughts so that he can move forward.

Ted takes some time after work and writes about his feelings in his journal. He begins with writing the following: *The reason I'm frustrated is because John got that promotion at work instead of me.* He looks at what he wrote and knows he needs to dig deeper. He knows he needs to identify the specific reason that not getting the promotion bothers him. He gives it another go. *I'm frustrated because now I'm not able to move to the next level in my calling as a business leader in this company.*

Now, he's getting somewhere.

He's identified the core reason at the root of these emotions, now all he needs to do is re-word it into a belief statement. After thinking about what he has written so far, he writes, *I believe that not getting this promotion is stopping me from being successful at living out my calling.*

At this point, Ted can review the truths he has learned and realize that whether or not he attains the promotion doesn't determine his success or failure at his calling. The fact that he is using his gifts, talents, and abilities to make the world a better place is what determines his success, not the attainment of a specific, temporal outcome. Ted pulls out this book, or maybe he reviews some highlighted sections in his journal from when he wrote down some light-bulb insights and revelations about calling and purpose. He reads them over again and again. He re-acquaints himself with the truth.

As he does so, he notices his perspective changes. His mind gets out of the rut of old thinking patterns and onto the road of right thinking about his calling and what it's all about. He begins to feel better, to again feel hopeful and excited about the opportunities that he has to exercise his calling. He writes in his journal: *What I have believed is a lie. The truth is that I can succeed every day at my calling whether or not I have that promotion. I still have opportunities to walk in my calling and no one can stop me from doing so. I choose to believe the truth and reject the lie. I choose to walk in my calling, and therefore I am succeeding.*

We'll touch on this process a bit more in the coming chapter as we add to the arsenal of truth that will help keep you on the right path. The journaling technique above is a great tool to help you whenever you feel like you've lost your momentum, or you're sliding back into the old beliefs. To start the process, just open your journal and write out the following question, filling in the blanks to align with your current emotional state:

I am feeling ____<fill in your emotions here>____.

Follow up that statement or group of statements with the following:

Why am I feeling ____<fill in your emotions here>____?

Then begin the next line with the below:

I am feeling ____<fill in your emotions here>____ because…

Now complete the sentence. But don't stop with just one sentence. Dig into it. Dredge up all those self-pitying, misguided, woe-is-me, I'm-a-failure-because feelings. Now is not the time to be pious and present the plastic-Jesus-face. It's time to be real. It's not time to analyze what you are writing. It's just time to vent. The analysis will come later. Right now, we just want the raw emotions and whatever comes into your brain. Once you're done, and you feel you've gotten it all down, put down your pen or shut the lid on your laptop and walk away.

Later—and 'later' could be anywhere from a few minutes to a few days afterward—come back and re-read what you wrote, and maybe even add to it if you need to. But once you're sure you have all the stuff that's rumbling around inside of you down on paper, you want to go to the next step. This is where you get to play detective to your own thought process. Read over everything you've written down so far and ask yourself, "What does this reveal about what I really believe?"

Now isn't the time to candy-coat anything. No one is going to judge you for admitting what you really believe. These are your private thoughts, and you don't have to share them with anyone else. You need to be brutally honest here. After you've thought about it, begin to write down the answer:

I believe ____<fill in the blank here>____.

In many cases you will probably have numerous belief statements by the time you finish this exercise, and that's fine.

These belief statements will help show you where your sub-conscious thinking has gotten off-track. It may take you pages and pages of journaling over weeks to finally drill down to the beliefs that are behind the negative emotions you experience when you don't reach a specific goal. Whether or not you can blow through the process in one afternoon, or whether or not it will take weeks, the process is the same. Eventually, with God's help, you can get to the point where you isolate your beliefs and, at that point, you will likely find the flaw in your thinking. Once you've done this, you can get about the business of re-ordering your thoughts to agree with the truth.

Finally, write out the truth:

The truth is ________________________.

Complete the sentence with the truth that corrects the lie you were getting sucked into. Then, meditate on it. Read it over and over again. Say it out loud. All of these actions help reinforce and deepen the neural pathways that must be built in order to establish a new way of thinking in your brain, a new way of living your life, a new belief that is in agreement with the truth.

I have found this technique to be a powerful tool to help me exchange incorrect thinking patterns and beliefs for the truth and right-thinking that can help lay the foundation for success and fulfillment. As you persist in this process of self-analysis and guiding your thought process in embracing the truth and rejecting the lies, I believe you will find that the frustration, disappointment, and other negative emotions will dissipate. Over time, you'll likely find yourself becoming more efficient at moving through the process, to the point where you can complete it all in your head in a few minutes.

No one likes a setback. No one likes to try accomplishing something and fall short of the mark. The trap comes when we equate failure to reach a specific secondary goal with failure to accomplish the primary goal of fulfilling our calling. Remember, fulfilling your calling is getting out there and using your gifts to make the world a better place, whether or not you get the outcome you were expecting or hoping for in the process.

Yes, you can change your beliefs

Belief is a choice. When I began my journey of transformation regarding what I believed about calling and success, I had a very different set of beliefs about these topics than I do now. I no longer believe the former misconceptions and half-truths because I chose, as an act of my will, to live differently. I chose, as an act of my will, to believe something different than what I had believed before. Yes, this change involved research, learning, prayer, and a good deal of mental exercise, but making the transition ultimately came down to making some straight-forward choices. I decided that A) I no longer wanted to live by my former beliefs regarding calling and success because they were not producing good results in my life, and B) I would choose to live by a new standard, a new definition of calling and success, as revealed in the Bible and understood through meditation, study, and hard work.

Summing it up

So far I've provided you a detailed plan for correctly defining success and given you some tools to help you change your old paradigm and adopt new beliefs. As your mindset begins to change, I think you'll find that it's a great relief to step off of the endless treadmill of pursuing accomplishment after accomplishment in order to prove your worth and validate your success. But this doesn't mean that all goals are bad or that we shouldn't measure performance. In the next chapter, we'll explore the healthy and productive use of goal-setting and measuring performance in this new paradigm.

Chapter 4 - On Setting Goals and Measuring Performance

For many of you, just reading the title of this chapter might have brought back a tight feeling in your chest or a knot in your stomach. Don't worry. We're not going back to try to re-package the failed strategy of using goals and measuring performance in order to define who we are and validate our self-worth. Instead, we're going to learn how to use these concepts as tools that will help us find more fulfillment and have a more significant impact in living out our calling—but without the guilt-inducing, soul-crushing feelings that often accompanied them in the past.

The purpose of goals

In a previous chapter, I mentioned the fact that our goals are not our god, and that treating them as such is part of the misguided mindset many of us start with as we begin this journey of transformation. But there is another side of the goals coin. Goals are not bad in and of themselves. In truth, goals are a necessary and vital part of successfully living out our calling. Goals are, fundamentally, *possibilities*. Goals help us paint a picture of what *might* happen. They can help motivate us and focus our efforts. So, what is the proper perspective we should have about setting and achieving (or sometimes falling short of) goals?

We've discussed the fact that a calling is defined as using our unique gifts, talents, and abilities to make the world a better place, and that we are a success at our calling any time we step out and attempt to do that. Think of this as your primary goal. Hopefully, you are learning to give yourself lots of grace in the process of living out your calling, and you are enjoying the journey. Yet, even though it's now a low-pressure goal (hopefully), it's still a goal. And even though I'm not operating in the old, negative my-performance-is-a-reflection-of-my-value-and-worth mindset, I continue to spend time, most days, sitting down at the keyboard to write or work on some other task related to my writing. In that sense, I measure my performance. In the same way that I don't get stressed out about getting dressed in the morning or brushing my teeth regularly, I don't stress out any more about the goal of living out my calling, either.

With the proper understanding of calling and success, we have learned that succeeding at living out the primary goal of our calling is not an impossible task. But there are many secondary goals that we set in the process of living out our primary goal which can be very difficult to achieve—goals that we sometimes fail to accomplish or only attain after a significant and prolonged effort. So, what's the right perspective to have when it comes to these secondary goals?

I can fulfill my calling every day by simply sitting down to write. But just doing this won't make me a best-selling author. Knowing the difference between the two types of goals is essential, and it can keep you from giving up when the hard work of pursuing secondary goals weighs upon you and the task you are trying to accomplish seems nearly impossible.

Thomas Edison invented the incandescent light bulb. It is difficult to over-estimate the profound positive effect his invention has had on human history. The computer I'm typing this manuscript on right now wouldn't exist if it weren't for the incandescent light bulb, for instance. And Thomas Edison was a world-class failure. That's right. While no one knows the exact number of experiments he conducted on his quest to invent the first commercially viable light bulb, it is clear that he failed at least a thousand times before finally perfecting the correct design (Rutgers School of Arts and Sciences, n.d.).

What was the attitude that enabled Edison to persevere in the face of repeated failure? It may have been the fact that he didn't see any of these experiments as failures at all. Once, while pursuing the development of a new type of storage battery, Edison and his chemists at Menlo Park attacked the design problems for five months, seven days a week, and performed over 9,000 (yes, nine thousand) experiments in the process. Edison's friend Walter S. Mallory said to Edison regarding the endeavor, "Isn't it a shame that with the tremendous amount of work you have done you haven't been able to get any results?" Mallory wrote of the reaction he received: "Edison turned on me like a flash, and with a smile replied: 'Results! Why, man, I have gotten lots of results! I know several thousand things that won't work!'" (ibid.).

Thomas Edison was called to be an inventor. To fulfill that calling, all he had to do was get up in the morning and use his gifts, talents, and abilities to pursue his desire to invent. This was a comparatively easy task when put next to the goal of inventing the light bulb or developing a new type of battery. The immediately tangible results from his efforts to invent on any particular day might have been amazing or disappointing. Still, the fact that he expended effort and brought his talents to bear in the process of doing so confirmed success at the primary goal of living out his calling. Inventing the incandescent lightbulb, however, was a much harder, secondary goal that he set for himself—and there was no guarantee he would achieve it. It took a long time, and there were many failed attempts.

Whatever your calling is, there are things you want to achieve in the process of living that calling out. There are dreams of becoming or doing that help fuel your passion. It is important to remember that, even though accomplishing these things might be very important to you, they are secondary goals. Some of them you will achieve, and some of them you probably won't achieve. God designed us to have goals and to be motivated to pursue them. As long as we don't make them idols that we believe determine our success or failure in and of themselves, they can help us instead of hinder us in our quest to live out our calling. So, what is the right perspective to have concerning these often hard-to-achieve goals?

Let's consider another example.

The young woman who feels a calling as an athlete may dream of being a professional basketball player one day. Her primary goal is to use her gifts, talents, and abilities in the field of athletics. Her secondary goal is to be a WNBA player someday. Thinking about reaching that secondary goal fuels her during long hours of grueling practice on and off of the court. Suppose, one day, while playing a game of basketball, she injures her knee in such a way that the career she's envisioned for herself is no longer possible. After all, this type of career-ending injury happens all of the time in sports.

Is this young woman now doomed to fail in living out her calling because of the career-ending injury? Hardly. She still has gifts, talents, and abilities. She is not doomed to fail in the goal of living out her calling—but she will likely need to find a new way to live out that calling besides becoming an NBA player. A new way of expressing her gifts, talents, and abilities must be found. She needs a *new secondary goal* to pursue. Maybe she becomes a coach now, instead of the player she dreamed of becoming. Maybe she pivots and instead invents a piece of protective gear that helps prevent the same type of injury she endured. Who knows? Failing to achieve the secondary goal doesn't stop her from being a success at her calling.

We all know people who failed to live up to their potential during some period of their lives. It may be because some tragedy motivated them to give up. It may be because they let a failure to achieve a specific secondary goal demoralize them and steal their passion. Or maybe it was an injury that made it physically impossible for them to pursue their calling in the same way that they had before. But none of these scenarios, or a hundred others that we could describe, is a calling-killer.

It is important to realize that God has equipped you with everything you need to be a success at your calling. All you need to do is choose to use the equipment and get into the game. The only person who can prevent you from fulfilling your calling is you.

At this point, you may be thinking, "*But I can't force people to buy my gadget, or read my book, or pick me to play on the hockey team, or (fill in the blank)*". True. But remember, that specific secondary goal—whatever it is—doesn't determine your success or failure at your calling.

It's not your primary goal.

We've all probably read inspiring stories or seen movies that inspire us to not give up on our dreams. One of my favorites of recent years is the story of Bethany Hamilton, a young girl who lost an arm in a shark attack, but battled back to become a champion surfer, despite the loss (Hamilton, 2006). Or the movie *The Blind Side* about Michael Oher, a homeless boy with a troubled family history who overcame the odds and went on to become a successful professional football player in the NFL. Yet, for every one of these stories, there are many other people whose goals drastically changed after they endured great tragedy or a significant setback. This second kind of story inspires us because the individual didn't let their failure to achieve one goal destroy their passion for fulfilling their calling. They found a way to use the same passion for their original goal to fuel the pursuit of something different. Without possibly understanding what they were doing, they were tapping into the truth that their calling was independent of that former goal.

Goals may change, and even a particular expression of your calling may change, but the fact that you have a calling never changes, and you can successfully pursue that calling no matter what setbacks you may face in life because you can always use the gifts, talents, and abilities that you have to try to make the world a better place. The choice is yours.

Use goals – don't let them use you.

Set secondary goals and pursue them, but realize they are simply tools that can help you live out the primary goal of your calling. Once that secondary goal is accomplished, you don't stop living out your calling—you pick a new secondary goal. If a particular goal isn't accomplished, you can set a new one, or you can continue to pursue the original goal, just like Thomas Edison did, until you either achieve it or die trying. Use goals to help motivate you and channel your efforts in a particular direction, but don't give them the power to defeat you.

Should we measure performance?

Measuring performance is a necessary part of life if we are at all concerned with improvement. What you don't measure, you usually don't improve upon.

We've talked a good bit about what it looks like to succeed at your primary goal of living out your calling, and in essence, how to measure such success. We simply look at our lives and ask ourselves, "Am I using my gifts, talents, and abilities to help make the world a better place?" If we can answer, "Yes," to that question, then we're living out our calling. How much time and effort you expend on doing that is between you and God, but I think a good rule of thumb is that you are spending some focused time on most days seeking to live that calling out in a practical way.

In this new paradigm of how we've discussed viewing calling and purpose, the measurement of success revolves around a relationship instead of a physically quantifiable measurement. It's not about counting how many widgets you sold or how many people are following you on social media. Instead, it's about the extent to which you've walked hand-in-hand and heart-to-heart with Jesus while you did whatever you've done.

At its base level, successfully fulfilling your calling and purpose is walking in communion with Jesus while you offer up your gifts, talents, and abilities to help make the world a better place. At the very core of this concept is the desire to let God's light shine through you and point to Him—however it is that you are uniquely equipped to do so.

That can't be quantified by a number. That can't be measured by a sales chart or a bank account. We can't put that in a jar and boast that we have more of it than someone else. It is personal, it is individual, and there is no way to take our bucket of accomplishments and compete with anyone else to prove we are 'better than' them.

The more we live in that head-space, the more we move away from traditional ways of measuring our success at our calling or purpose, the more peace and fulfillment we will have, and the more freedom we will experience in living out our calling. The less afraid we are of falling short, the more secure we are in the truth that God already approves of us and will never love us more or less based upon our accomplishments or performance. The more fully we embrace this truth, the more free we become to let His light shine through us in our own unique way. And living in this mindset really will make the world the best place it can possibly be.

But that's not the end of the story, is it? There are all of these secondary goals we have that are unique to us. And some of these goals are big and require a lot of planning and effort to achieve. So, how do I measure my success in pursuing these goals? Do I measure myself against others? Do I deem myself more or less successful based on some external, temporal measure of success involving the number of social media followers, the size of my bank account, or how many people bought the widgets that I made last week?

There's nothing wrong with measuring how far we've come to achieving a particular goal. The problem arises when we use that measurement as a barometer that determines our level of success in living out our calling. Remember, there is a difference between reaching secondary goals and being a success at living out your calling. They are not the same.

Suppose I'm using a new marketing strategy designed to sell more widgets or reach more people with my message. After a while, it turns out that I only reached half of the people that I targeted or sold half of the widgets I intended to sell. In short, I didn't reach that particular goal. The only way I will know this is if I measure it. However, whether or not I reach that particular goal has nothing to do with whether or not I was successful at my primary goal of living out my calling.

There are many books and articles out there that can teach you how to plan and achieve goals. I won't attempt to replicate that information here. Using those tools to help achieve a secondary goal is perfectly fine as long as you keep the right perspective regarding what your primary and secondary goals are. When pursuing secondary goals, it is important to stay focused on the primary goal of your calling and how to define success in that endeavor. Keeping your mind and heart grounded firmly in the reality of your identity in Christ Jesus will help you keep the right balance in this process.

You may want to earn a 4.0 in your chemistry class as part of your calling to be a chemist. If you got a 'C' on your last test, it's worthwhile to be able to admit that you need to increase your study-time from one hour a day to two hours a day in order to achieve that goal. And, if, after doing that, you make a 'B' on the next test, you may need to make additional investments in order to achieve an 'A'. For some who try this, the 'A' might not be possible this time around. Shooting for the 'A' and getting the 'B' is a failure to get an 'A', but a success in improving on a 'C'! Much of success or failure at a task is how you choose to look at it.

Keep in mind the perspective that we've discussed in this chapter when you measure your performance. If you follow this advice, then goal-setting and performance measurement will help you rather than hinder you in your journey of living out your calling. With this understanding of how goals and performance fit into your calling, we're now ready to add the final piece to the puzzle and discuss God's winning strategy for long-term success at living out your calling.

So far, we've identified a plan for correctly defining success and given you some tools to help you adopt new beliefs. But these alone will not guarantee that you will live out your calling successfully in the long run. This journey isn't a sprint for a few months. This is a lifelong marathon. I want you to reach the finish line of this life in a full-on, passionate pursuit of your calling. And to do that, you need more than help getting started—you need a long-term strategy for success that will stand the test of time.

You need a strategy that can accommodate anything life may toss at you. In the next chapter, we'll examine God's plan for doing just that.

In order to reach the finish line of this life in a full-on passionate pursuit of your calling, you need a long-term strategy for success that will stand the test of time and endure anything life may toss at you. You need to know God's strategy for success. It brings together everything we've talked about so far, putting it into a cohesive game plan that is a winning blueprint designed by God to ensure your effectiveness at bringing your unique expression of calling to full bloom on the Earth. God is on your side. He wants you to succeed.

God's strategy for successfully fulfilling your calling

Once you determine how you are going to use the gifts, talents, and abilities that God has given you in order to make the world a better place, the battle is not over. In fact, it has just shifted into a new phase. You may be serving in a homeless ministry, visiting the elderly in nursing homes, pursuing that manager's position at your job, working on furthering your education, or writing a novel—whatever it is, you will undoubtedly face challenges.

We could face persecution from others in the form of hate or doubt, or even physical resistance. Whatever form it comes in, this resistance, whether passive or active, is a force that works against what we are attempting to accomplish. How we handle this resistance, not the resistance itself, is the dragon that we must slay if we want to succeed at our calling long-term. If we fail in this task, choosing instead to either give up on our calling altogether or taking a path of less resistance and ceasing to push the boundaries, then we can easily fall short of our potential.

Many stories in the Bible show us people living out their callings and accomplishing tremendous things. In every one of these stories, the person in question has to overcome great obstacles and challenges in order to reach their goal. Paul endured years in a prison cell while writing two-thirds of the New Testament. Joseph endured years of slavery after unwisely taunting his brothers with tales of his God-given calling before finally being exalted to Pharaoh's right hand. Mary had to endure the social shame of being an unwed mother and the short-term rejection of her future husband Joseph before giving birth to Jesus, the Christ. In each of these stories, there was a point and time where it would have been easier for them to give up than to persevere in faith and continue to pursue their God-given calling.

But instead of failing, they succeeded. They succeeded because they were employing God's strategy for success, whether they knew it or not. Some of them didn't have it down pat at first. In fact, some of them started out doing everything wrong. But eventually, each of them began to implement God's winning strategy—and it enabled them to live out their calling successfully and achieve great things.

As I learned these truths for myself, I reached a point where it became apparent that I was likely years away from realizing some of my goals—if they were ever to be realized at all. I had repeatedly modified my expected timelines. After each modification, new understanding and experience taught me that I still might have been overly optimistic in measuring the probability of my success at achieving certain goals. Eventually, I came to the conclusion that I might fall far short of what I'd initially envisioned, and that I might not achieve some of these goals at all.

Why had I arrived at this point? Because there was opposition to me achieving my goals.

There were things standing in my way that I had little or no control over and which made achieving the goals I had set much more difficult than I had previously imagined. If you've lived long enough to set many goals in life, you understand the concept. You are not guaranteed to reach every goal you strive for. The bigger the goal, the greater the obstacles to achieving the goal, and the more effort required to attain it.

By this point in my journey, I had already begun to learn that my goals were not my god, and that success in pursuing the primary goal of my calling was not hinged on achieving a specific set of secondary goals. But I still felt tempted to throw in the towel, to lay these goals aside and pick some goals that I considered more realistic. I was feeling discouraged and drained of passion at the thought of all the hard work and possibly years of waiting that might be required before I would see these goals come to fruition—if, indeed, they ever would.

But opposition from external forces wasn't the only obstacle in my path. I began to question whether pursuing my calling was accomplishing anything worthwhile. I didn't doubt my calling; I started doubting whether or not it mattered that I pursued my calling.

Sometimes when we are pursuing a secondary goal and we're facing the long, hard battle with opposing forces—whatever they may be—we can begin to question our impact. We can start to doubt. You may question your effectiveness. Are you really making a difference? Is the choice you are making to spend your time pursuing goal 'X' really better than just going to the beach to get a tan or going surfing? These doubts, if left un-dealt with, can eventually lead you to give up on pursuing your calling.

Don't let that happen to you.

When I reached this place, I knew I needed something more than the revelations on calling and success that I had already obtained to help me stay in the game and not give up. As I continued to journal and pray, and read God's Word and wrestle with the situation, God's still small voice whispered into my soul the first piece of His strategy for success. I can remember sitting in my chair, contemplating the obstacles that seemed so daunting, and wondering how I was ever going to overcome them. Then a single thought came into my mind that I knew had been placed there by God's Holy Spirit.

You need to have faith.

It was a simple phrase, but it was just what I needed to hear. I didn't just need to come up with a better action plan. I needed to have faith. I needed to be able to believe in something more than what I could see or plan for or put on paper.

But faith in what? Faith that I would achieve the goals I had set? That still didn't sit right with me. We sometimes fail to achieve specific goals. Putting my faith in achieving a goal that I might not attain in the end had been part of my initial problem when I'd begun this journey to discover my calling. Surely, that wasn't it.

As I pondered this question, I came across a story of one of Jesus' miracles that provided the insight I needed. It was the parable of the boy with the five loaves and two fishes (John, Chapter 6). You may remember it. Jesus has preached all day. Thousands of people are gathered to hear him, and it is getting late. The people are hungry. Jesus tells the disciples to feed them, and they are dumbfounded. "With what?" they ask. A small boy witnesses this exchange and does something only a child would do—he offers up his small lunch to Jesus in answer to the question. He gives God his five loaves and two fish. That little boy didn't know exactly what Jesus was going to do with his meager offering, but he believed Jesus could use what he was offering to help meet a need that was much greater than he could meet on his own.

The boy could have simply turned to a neighbor who hadn't brought anything with them to eat, and offered to share what he had with that one person. That would have been kind—loving, even. But when he heard that Jesus had told his disciples to feed the whole crowd, his heart leapt. He wanted to be part of that. He didn't stop to figure out how, but he knew that giving what little he had to this man Jesus was the place to start.

And Jesus takes this little boy's small offering and performs a great miracle.

The meager resources the boy had are multiplied and used to feed thousands of people, with leftovers to spare.

And then I got it. God wasn't trying to get me to have faith in what ***I*** could do. He wasn't trying to get me to adopt an if-I-just-try-harder-or-work-smarter-then-it-will-work attitude. God wanted me to have faith in what ***He*** could do with whatever I brought to the table.

The world needs the full expression of your unique calling brought to bear in order to bring God's kingdom here on Earth. There are people and situations that you can affect in your own unique way, which no one else will be able to affect like you can. Just because there are times when you're blinded to that fact doesn't mean it isn't true. Have faith. Press on. Don't give up.

There will always be a challenge that is bigger than us which we will need to overcome in the process of pursuing our calling. It wouldn't be a God-given calling if there weren't. Dreaming about doing something beyond what we can reasonably expect to accomplish on our own is part of living out our God-given calling. Step one in what God wanted me to do with the obstacles I was facing was to have faith in what He could do with my own five loaves and two fish. I only needed to believe that God could take what I was bringing to the table and work a miracle.

Once I embraced this faith-filled attitude, my attitude began to improve. Suddenly, I didn't have to solve all of the problems that I thought needed to be addressed. I didn't have to figure out a plan to feed the five thousand. I didn't have to figure out every step of how I was going to use my gifts, talents, and abilities to be a success at living out my calling. For me, that meant I didn't have to have a ten-step, bullet-proof plan to increasing my reader base to 'X' number of people. I just needed to keep writing and putting my work out there, using the tools and knowledge that I had available at the time, and trust God with the rest. That was me bringing my five loaves and two fishes to Jesus. Not focusing on what I couldn't do, but focusing on what I *could* do and trusting God to take that and use it to help perform a miracle.

For the person whose calling is to be the best mom you can be at this point in your life, that means you don't have to have the answer right now for how to help your kid overcome that anger problem. Certainly, you need to apply yourself to do what you *can* do—read books, seek wise counsel, pray, and put what you learn into practice—then trust God with the results. Keep looking to God and expecting Him to provide help. And He will. God will come through. You don't have to do it all on your own. Your calling isn't a solo act. It's you and God working together. So, hold on, press on in faith, and don't give up.

The next part of God's winning strategy is opposition. Yes, that's right. You didn't read that wrong, and I didn't make a typo. Yes, it's true that Satan wants to use opposition to destroy you and prevent you from successfully living out your calling. But God's plan doesn't involve removing all opposition from your life. Instead, He intends to use the obstacles in your life to help make you unstoppable, to enable you to live out your calling no matter what gets thrown at you along the way. Now, I ask you, between God and the Devil, who do you think has the winning insight on opposition?

How God uses opposition to your advantage

In the Bible, another word that connotes this idea of opposition is 'tribulation'. Consider the following passage from Romans 5:3-5 (NASB):

> ***And not only this, but we also exult in our tribulations,***

> ***knowing that tribulation brings about perseverance; and perseverance, proven character; and proven character, hope; and hope does not disappoint, because the love of God has been poured out within our hearts through the Holy Spirit who was given to us.***

Did you catch that? Facing tribulation—opposition—and pushing through it, produces something. It produces perseverance, character, and hope. These are all characteristics that we need to develop and strengthen if we are to pursue our calling successfully.

There is a unique phenomenon in space travel called microgravity bone loss. When an astronaut spends a certain amount of time in space, their bones start becoming weaker, more brittle (Sutton, 2005). This phenomenon occurs because, in space, there is no gravity. No gravity means your bones don't have the resistance of your body weight acting against them. They have no opposition. And this, it turns out, is a bad thing. This phenomenon causes some biological switch to turn off that is required to make the bones strong. So, the bones become brittle. Once back on Earth, with gravity acting on their bodies once again, the weak bones make these former astronauts more prone to breaks. (ibid.)

Anyone who has ever been an athlete or worked out to make their body stronger knows about this principle. You want to become stronger so you can lift more weight? In addition to good nutrition and adequate sleep, you need to lift a series of increasingly heavier weights over a period of time. If a reasonably healthy individual does this, they will be stronger in the end, able to lift heavier weights than they could when they started their weightlifting regimen.

God allows opposition into our lives to make us strong enough to overcome more significant obstacles down the line. He's using opposition to train us. But instead of bigger muscles, it produces perseverance, character, and hope. If we endure the opposition that we are currently experiencing in the process of pursuing our calling, if we endure it in faith, then God's training will produce the intended result. We don't have to overcome the opposition; we simply have to endure it and refuse to give up. God will provide a way out at the right time if we just don't give up.

There are many examples in nature where pressure exerted upon a thing produces something far more valuable than what would exist if the pressure were absent. The most notable example of this is the diamond. Without the intense pressure put on a lump of coal by the Earth, diamonds would not exist. The beauty of the diamond is matched by its incredible hardness—both of which are the result of pressure.

In the realm of human-made things, pressure can also be of tremendous value. Pressure-treated wood, for instance, is often used for construction projects that will leave the wood exposed to the elements. The pressure-treating infuses the wood with chemicals to prevent rotting, which enables this wood to last for years longer than untreated wood.

Just like in these examples, the pressure we face to quit, give up, or sell out as we pursue our calling can actually help prepare us to go the distance and out-last the forces that oppose us. When we face these obstacles and allow God to shepherd us through them, we come out of the process stronger and better able to maximize our impact for God's kingdom and finish this life well.

Think of a team sport like football. The players of the same team often hold practice games where they play against each other. The players get pushed around, tackled, and sometimes injured in these practice games. The punishment they endure on the practice field is the preparation that the team needs if they are to win the real game. So, too, the opposition we experience as we pursue our calling is allowed by God, Who uses it to help shape us into something more beautiful and more durable than we could ever be without it.

That's what God's plan is for allowing opposition into our lives. It's there to make us stronger so that we can go on to do even greater things. If we face opposition in faith, realizing that we will need God's assistance to overcome it, knowing that assistance will come when we need it, then we have the second part of God's winning strategy for success.

In the next chapter, we'll take a look at the final two components of God's plan—focus and results.

Chapter 6 - Focus and Results

There is one characteristic that every successful person I know shares. They demonstrate the ability to focus on the relentless pursuit of a thing. Be they a sports figure, politician, writer, teacher, baker, business owner, mother, or father—those who are successful at what they do demonstrate the ability to consistently focus on a set of actions that will move them forward towards a goal.

The next part of God's winning strategy for success is focus.

In implementing God's plan to succeed at your calling, you need to consistently focus on Who you are pursuing this calling for in the first place. When the going gets tough, it will be more tempting to give up if you think pursuing your calling is all about you and your temporal happiness. In reality, it is about much more than that.

God is depending on you to live out your calling as an integral part of His plan to bring the kingdom of God to Earth. There are people you will be able to affect in your lifetime, in specific places and times, with your unique gifts, talents, and abilities, whom no one else will be able to affect in the same way. This gives you a unique opportunity to help mold the future that no one else could possibly take advantage of. It is yours alone. And God has no 'Plan B' for doing that if you choose not to cooperate with Him in that effort. If you believe that, then your focus should—first and foremost—be on Him. Do everything as if you were doing it for Jesus. After all, it is God Who you serve and it is from Him that you will receive your eternal reward (Colossians 3:23-24).

God called you so you could work together with Him to help make the world a better place. It's about relationship—the whole reason for why we were created in the first place. A person in passionate pursuit of their calling while walking hand-in-hand with God is the fulfillment of God's purpose in creating humankind.

The second thing you will need to focus on consistently, if you want to succeed, is a plan.

There is a saying, "You can't steer a parked car." This idea certainly applies to successfully living out your calling. No plan you will ever develop in life will be a perfect plan, but pursuing any plan is a way to get you moving towards a goal. And if you are moving towards the goal of living out your calling and you are in constant relationship with God, then He can help you course-correct and adjust your plan so that it becomes a better and better plan over time.

You can understand everything in this book, and yet, if you fail to do this one thing, you will fall far short of the potential God has placed in you as you live out your calling. I encourage you to take the following steps to heart:

1. Have a plan.
2. Work the plan.
3. Make adjustments to the plan as needed.

Don't get hung up on having the perfect plan. Remember those people in the Bible who we look up to because they fulfilled their calling in life? None of them except Jesus ever had a perfect plan to do so. Moses botched his first plan to live out his calling as a deliverer so badly that he ended up having to flee Egypt as a man wanted for murder. Not a great plan. Abraham wavered in his calling to be the father of God's chosen offspring and came up with his own plan to help God out, spawning centuries of conflict between two of his offspring and their descendants—a conflict that continues today. Paul thought up a plan in his zeal to serve God that started with killing Christians—you can't come up with a worse plan than that! But in each of these case, and in many others throughout history, God turned the situation around. In the end, these men ended up accomplishing great things as they lived out their calling in relationship with a loving and all-powerful God Who directed their steps. God has continued to direct the lives of countless other men and women throughout history in this same way, and He will do so in your life if you will invite Him to do so. Take encouragement from the words of Proverbs 16:9 (NASB), which says: "The mind of man plans his way, but the LORD directs his steps."

The key to this part of the focus step of God's strategy for success is not to have the perfect plan, but to have some kind of plan for living out your calling and taking consistent steps to work that plan. You can have the best plan in the world, but if you never implement it, you won't accomplish anything. Take that first step in trying to implement a plan to live out your calling, then the next, and the next. Somewhere along the way—if you are listening—God will reveal some wisdom to help you modify your plan and be more effective in living out your calling.

Don't get caught in 'analysis paralysis' when it comes to developing your plan. Also, don't shoot from the hip and come up with a plan in five minutes without thinking it through. Take some time to do your research. Pray. Seek the counsel of others who may be knowledgeable about the thing you are attempting to do. But don't take ten years to plan. Thirty days should be sufficient to come up with a basic plan, even if part of that plan involves more planning! Then, begin to work the steps of the plan consistently over time.

Suppose you are an engineer, and you feel a calling to use your gifts differently than you do in your current job, but you're not sure how to go about it. A good suggestion is to begin with research. There are a number of organizations that conduct short-term missions for professionals with engineering abilities. You may even find a particular organization that you want to consider working for full-time. After you've researched the possibilities for a few weeks, take another week to come up with a plan of action. You may decide you need another thirty days of research before you come up with other action steps, or you may determine that the next step is to contact one of these organizations and begin the process of scheduling a short-term mission trip.

Maybe you love to bake and feel it is your calling—to bless others through making good food. You think you might include encouraging Bible verses on cards attached to the wrapping. Take a week or two to decide how you will begin this task. How will you identify the recipients of your baked goods? Will you sell them, or simply give them away, or both? How will you fund this project? Once you've come up with a plan, then begin working the steps, and bake that first cake and get it to someone who will be blessed with it!

Just like God allows most of us to discover our calling as part of a process that usually doesn't include an angelic visitation, the same is true with planning how to pursue our calling. And just like in the parable of the talents, God has given you these gifts, talents, and abilities, and He doesn't always provide specific instructions on exactly how to use them. If you've followed the advice presented in the first book in this series, you've hopefully learned how to navigate the process of determining your specific calling by now (if you're still in the process of doing so, don't lose heart! Keep pressing on!). These same principles apply to creating a plan to live out your calling. Take time to pray and listen to what God might be directing you to do. Ask Him to help guide your steps. And then use the brain and other resources He has provided you with to set some goals and make a plan to reach those goals. Then work the plan, revising as needed.

Remember, you aren't responsible for coming up with the perfect plan. You are responsible for pursuing your calling—for using your gifts, talents, and abilities to make the world a better place. As you step out in faith and begin to do that, God will help you with the planning part along the way. He's an expert at taking bad plans and turning them into good plans.

Lastly, (and this is important) leave the results up to God.

Moses had a plan. He didn't yet know the God of Jacob, but he had a desire deep within his soul to help deliver the Israelites from their cruel Egyptian taskmasters. It was his calling, although he might not have known it at the time. We don't really know what Moses was thinking that day when he saw the Egyptian mistreating one of his Hebrew brothers. I can imagine the anger that welled up inside of him at witnessing, for the thousandth time, an Egyptian beating a Hebrew slave. While we don't know what his thoughts were in those moments, we know how they ended up changing his life. Motivated by his desire to live out his calling, Moses came up with a bad plan, likely on the spur of the moment. He looked around quickly and didn't see anyone else to witness what he was about to do, and then he killed the Egyptian who was mistreating the Hebrew. Afterwards, he buried the Egyptian's body in the sand and went on about his business.

Moses' rash actions ultimately led to him fleeing Egypt as a man wanted for murder, and spending the next forty years on the backside of the wilderness herding sheep.

How's that for a great plan to successfully live out your calling?

But God had a purpose, even in allowing Moses to implement his horribly misguided plan. You see, God knew something Moses didn't. God knew that Moses' character wasn't ready to help deliver the Israelites. This brash, self-assured prince of Egypt was too self-confident and arrogant, at the age of forty, to be the kind of deliverer that God had in mind to demonstrate His power and deliver the Hebrews from Egyptian bondage. What he needed was a king-sized dose of humility. And God allowed Moses to follow his own misguided plan to murder the Egyptian that day, using the horrible outcome to, ultimately, help develop humility in Moses.

Fast-forward forty years. Moses is now eighty. No longer the brash and arrogant young prince of Egypt. Being a herder of sheep for forty years has taught him humility. The Bible says that, at this point in his life, Moses was the most humble man on Earth (Numbers 12:3). It was then that God decided that Moses was ready to fulfill his calling. It was then, at the sight of a burning bush that would not be consumed, that God presented Himself to Moses and revealed His plan for Moses to help deliver the Israelites from bondage.

The results of Moses' first action plan to live out his calling were a disaster by his standards, but God used those results to help set up the eventual and spectacular fulfillment of Moses calling—forty years later.

What's the point here?

The point is that, when we come up with a plan to achieve a goal, we usually have a precise idea of what it will look like if we are successful in achieving that goal. Our child will see the light of our wisdom and study harder, thereby earning better grades and getting into the college of our… err… *their* dreams. We'll study hard after work for that real-estate exam, pass the exam, and then go on to earn a better living. We'll confront our spouse about their gambling problem, they'll see the light and get the help they need, and our family will be made whole again.

Whatever our plans are, we don't just have a plan; we have a specific idea of what the results will look like if the plan is successful. But that isn't always what happens. Sometimes people fail the exam, the spouse chooses divorce, or the kid flunks out. Sometimes, our plan fails to achieve the desired results.

But God knows before we begin implementing our plan exactly how it is going to work out. So, why doesn't He tell us? Why doesn't He clue us in so that we can make the course corrections before we mess things up, or at least avoid investing in a bad plan that other people and situations beyond our control are going to mess up?

Because God has a better plan, and sometimes it involves the failure of our plans.

If Moses had gotten away with murder, do you think that would have led him to become the humble leader that he eventually became? I don't think so. Our failures can become tools in the hands of the Almighty, which He can then use to fashion our characters and ultimately enable us to be more successful at fulfilling our calling. If we trust God with the results of our plans, then we won't get so discouraged and disheartened on the journey. We are not in this alone. God is working with us, and He knows what He's doing.

I had plans to write a great novel, succeed at selling thousands of copies, and become the next great American novelist within five years. But if that plan had worked as intended, I wouldn't have learned the principles that will help you find and fulfill your own calling, and you wouldn't be reading these words right now.

God had a better plan, and it required me to fail at mine.

God's better plans for us required that Moses fail at his plan. God's ultimate plans require that we all fail at some level, and repeatedly, as we are living out our various callings in life. And that's a good thing. We simply need to trust that, whether our plans succeed the way we want them to or not, God can take our five loaves and two fishes, or our bankrupt business, or our failure to pass that exam, and use it all to perform a miracle. And if we trust God with the results of what our plans are or will produce, then we have the final piece of God's plan.

God's strategy for success in review

Let's review God's strategy for success now that we've discussed all of the parts:

1) Faith – Have faith in God to guide your steps, and take your five loaves and two fishes and do something amazing with them. He will if you will let Him.
2) Perseverance – God uses opposition and obstacles in your journey of living out your calling as tools to help develop your ability to persevere. As you learn to persevere, good character and hope grow inside of you. So don't give up. Keep living out your calling!

3) Focus – There are two parts to the focus step.
    a. Focus on Who you are pursuing this calling for in the first place (that would be God). Walking in fellowship with Him at every step of your journey is the point. Remember—calling is about relationship, not just doing or becoming something. God wants to be in continual communion with you on this journey.
    b. Focus on the plan for how you will use your gifts, talents, and abilities to make the world a better place (a.k.a. living out your calling).
        i. Make a plan.
        ii. Work the plan.

iii. Revise the plan as needed.

4) Trust God with the results. Remember that the plan you are following isn't always going to produce the results you desire at the time you desire them. Don't get side-tracked by what may appear at first to be disappointing results. God has a purpose in how things turn out that you may not understand. In time, you will begin to see His perspective on perceived failures or unexpected results. Sometimes our most significant failures are a setup from God that can lead to our greatest triumphs. And when the good results start showing up, don't forget to thank God for helping bring them about!

In Conclusion

It's been a whirlwind journey that we've taken together. I pray that this book has been a help to you and inspired you in some way. If so, don't forget to share what you've learned with someone else—because God wants everyone to live a fulfilling life doing what they are called to do. The world needs this gift from all of us.

And now, as I write these concluding thoughts, I have some closing advice that will hopefully serve as a giant shove-off for your canoe as you continue your voyage.

Each action we take is a seed.

Every time we use our gifts, talents, and abilities in an attempt to make the world a better place, we are planting a seed, the potential of which we cannot possibly fathom. You might share a kind word with a stranger that encourages them to hang on one more day and refuse to commit suicide, and that stranger may then go on to do other good deeds themselves and so on. The act of graciously letting someone get in front of you in traffic may inspire them with a glimmer of God's love in an otherwise stressful day. You may encourage a co-worker by saying, 'good job' and help them find a bit of fulfillment and validation in a challenging work environment. Like so many grains of sand, each act of goodness is building towards the revelation of God's kingdom here on Earth, the revelation of His glory and love.

Don't give in to discouragement. Choose to live in faith, not in doubt. Keep sowing those seeds of God's love that can only come as you use your unique gifts, talents, and abilities to help make the world a better place.

Choose to persist in faith. Understand that you are not alone in offering your five loaves and two fishes. Understand that, whatever you accomplish or attempt to accomplish, you are doing so in concert with a loving, all-powerful God Who can take your meager offerings and perform something miraculous with them.

Did Jesus need the five loaves and two fishes given by that small boy so that He could feed the five thousand? Technically, no. But He *chose* to need it. God created you so that He could experience living life *with* you, not in spite of you. Your greatest gift to God is joining Him in bringing His kingdom here on Earth by using your gifts, talents, and abilities to assist in that effort. It is the communion that occurs as you join Him in that journey that brings Him joy. Two hearts - yours and His - joined in the act of spreading God's love in the way you are uniquely gifted to do so. It is music to the Father's ears and brings joy to His Spirit. It is the reason God created humankind to begin with.

And it will require faith.

It will require that we struggle at times.

It will require perseverance.

It will require that we overcome self-doubt, discouragement, and other obstacles. But with God's help, and the help of those who God places along our path to aid us, we can succeed at the task if we want to.

I pray you will be blessed with much success on your journey.

Milliot, Jim (2019). Number of Self-Published Titles Jumped 40% in 2018. Publishers Weekly. Retrieved February 6, 2020 from https://www.publishersweekly.com/pw/by-topic/industry-news/publisher-news/article/81473-number-of-self-published-titles-jumped-40-in-2018.html

Rutgers School of Arts and Sciences. (n.d.). Myth Buster: Edison's 10,000 attempts. Rutgers.edu. Retrieved April 9, 2020 from http://edison.rutgers.edu/newsletter9.html#4

Sutton, Jeffrey (2005). How does spending prolonged time in microgravity affect the bodies of astronauts? Scientific American. Retrieved April 10, 2020 from https://www.scientificamerican.com/article/how-does-spending-prolong/

Acknowledgements

Thanks to the many beta readers of this work for their helpful comments, suggestions, and input. Thanks to my editor, whose work and comments helped to make this a better book. To be fair to her, any mistakes you may find are likely at the points I decided not to take her editing suggestions.

About the Author

C.L. Wells lives with his family in Charleston County, South Carolina. His hobbies include writing non-fiction, Murder Mystery, YA, Paranormal, and Crime/Adventure fiction, paddle boarding, hiking, and bicycling.

For up to date information on the latest releases and upcoming books, visit **www.fictionwithamission.com**.

GET YOUR FREE BOOK:
http://fictionwithamission.com/go/free-book

www.ingramcontent.com/pod-product-compliance
Lightning Source LLC
LaVergne TN
LVHW091250150826
845673LV00006B/1380
9798685980533